Timing the Real Estate Market

How to Buy Low and Sell High in Real Estate

Craig Hall

McGraw-Hill
New York   Chicago   San Francisco   Lisbon
London   Madrid   Mexico City   Milan   New Delhi
San Juan   Seoul   Singapore   Sydney   Toronto

ISBN 0-07-142195-5

Editorial and production services provided by CWL Publishing Enterprises, Inc., Madison, Wisconsin, www.cwlpub.com.

This publication is designed to provide accurate and authoritative information in regard to the subject matter covered. It is sold with the understanding that neither the author nor the publisher is engaged in rendering legal, accounting, or other professional service. If legal advice or other expert assistance is required, the services of a competent professional person should be sought.

> —*From a Declaration of Principles jointly adopted*
> *by a Committee of the American Bar*
> *Association and a Committee of Publishers*

McGraw-Hill books are available at special quantity discounts to use as premiums and sales promotions, or for use in corporate training programs. For more information, please write to the Director of Special Sales, McGraw-Hill, Two Penn Plaza, New York, NY 10121-2298, or contact your local bookstore.

 This book is printed on recycled, acid-free paper containing a minimum of 50% recycled de-inked fiber.

Contents

Contents

Acknowledgments

When I was 27 years old, Tom Connellan, a close friend and respected author, suggested to his publisher that they hire me to write a book. By then I was entering my tenth year in the real estate business and had become known for turning around financially distressed properties. At Tom's urging Prentice Hall, and in particular an editor named Ted Nardin, took a risk on me as an unproven author. *The Real Estate Turnaround*, published in 1978, was the first of five books that I have now written.

In my career as an author—that is, until this book—I would generally take (and need) a number of years off after completing each book. The truth be told, once I completed each one, I would say, "Never again!" Writing books is not a pleasure for me. While it is true that I enjoy sharing ideas and information, writing is lonely, hard work.

Ted Nardin is now a senior executive at McGraw-Hill. It was Ted who originally suggested to one of McGraw-Hill's editors that I be contacted to write a book about real estate. After speaking with Richard Narramore and being flattered by his interest, I decided to ignore my "Never again!" promise and prepare a proposal in response. I worked hard to come up with what I thought would be an interesting real estate book, and Richard and I developed a good working relationship in the process. My proposal was approved at the first committee level, but turned down at the second. These things happen, and I long ago learned to take disappointments in stride and move on.

Acknowledgments

Richard felt badly that the book hadn't worked out—especially since he had gained a sense of what was unique about my real estate career. It wasn't long until Richard contacted me again and suggested I write a book on timing the real estate market. It was his belief, and I certainly agree, that readers could benefit from knowing more about this subject. He actually generated some of the first outlines and presented me with the concept and related details. This time both of the McGraw-Hill committees approved the proposal. *Richard, thank you for the willingness, creativeness, and perseverance it took to birth this project!* Richard also deserves great credit and acknowledgment for his ongoing and consistent role in guiding the work as well as his detailed edit of the final manuscript.

The writing of this book has been a team effort. My early rough first drafts were challenged, edited, rewritten, and discussed in depth with Lisa Boyer and Mark Blocher. Lisa owns and runs a company that has been Hall Financial Group's outside public relations firm for years. Her tireless efforts, insights, and detailed writing skills have been invaluable to this project. Mark's "day job" is Director of Corporate Communications for Hall Financial Group. He and I have worked together since 1984, giving him the advantage of having lived through much of my education on timing the real estate markets. Mark's ability to cut through confusion and help crystallize concepts has been critical. He has worked tirelessly, giving up nights and weekends to further this project. Together the three of us worked on at least 15 to 20 draft versions of every section in the book.

The more finished editing of the book was accomplished in stages. An excellent writer who helped me with several of my past books, Sally Stephenson, was responsible for the first rewrites during the final polishing stage. For a detailed review of grammar (but more importantly whether the words would make sense to a new reader), our In-House Counsel, Melinda Jayson, has read, reread, and edited on a thorough basis. My wife Kathryn has also been helpful, by reading, editing, and providing me with her candid and trusted opinions.

Acknowledgments

Others who assisted in various stages of the editing process include Mark LaCourse, Mike Jaynes, and David Nachman.

Kimberly Forbes, my assistant in California, typed portions of the early drafts and various chapter edits. But the majority of the transcribing and typing (and retyping of most of the entire manuscript over and over again) was accomplished by Barbara Milo, my Executive Assistant at our home office in Frisco, Texas. Barbara spent many weeknights and weekends transcribing dictated works and redoing edited works. Last, but not least, thanks go to David Nachman, who turned my scribbled notes on paper into charts that could actually be understood.

While I am deeply grateful to all those who actively brought this book from idea to completion, there are so many others who directly or indirectly have played a role in my learning about timing. I am extremely blessed to be surrounded by a group of fantastic associates—many of whom have worked with me for 25 years or more. We have all learned and literally grown up together, often through tough and expensive lessons. Some of my associates at Hall Financial go back with me as far as the 1960s. Mark Depker, who today is President of our management company, began working with me as a maintenance man in 1969 on one of my first larger property acquisitions. Don Braun, President of Hall Financial Group, and Larry Levey, President of our development division, are key long-term senior executives and partners with me in our many timing lessons. In addition, the following individuals have all been with me at Hall Financial Group for over 15 years. Each one of them in their own unique way deserves thanks for helping us collectively learn what is taught in this book about timing the real estate markets. My personal thanks go to Karen Sucher, Daniel Wand, Mary Lee Miller, Paul Zak, Mike Bawulski, Masten Harris, Danny Eversole, Terri Leirstein, Howard Misener, Ricky Anderson, Valerie Reber, Deloris White, Tammy McGuire, Craig Thornsbury, Sharon Young, Francisco Renteria, Margarita Fabian, George Fiedorczyk, Sandra Conley, Keith Taylor, Marla Pearson, Janet

Acknowledgments

Roznowski, Marian Nolan-Neville, Jan McCain, Nydia Lopez, Federico Albavera, Ida Young, Linda Bowlin, Pat Murray, Judy Martin, Sally Miller, Angela Berggren, Bruce Wagner, Jose Avelar, Patricia Buffington, Linda Moak, Beverly Sink, Wesley Sink, James Burke, Linda Hogden, Mikel Dubose, and David Epperson.

There are many others who for varying reasons no longer work with us but who were great contributors for many years. By way of recognizing some, but certainly not all, I owe special thanks to Tom Jahncke, Mike Kilbourn, Bob Cohen, Peter Nunez, Robert Flynn, Marti Kohnke, and Beth Mooney. To all these and to the many others who are so deserving of my appreciation and gratitude, I say thank you.

The ups and downs of my journey over these past 35 years would not have been the same anywhere else in the world. Where else could a 17-year-old take $4,000, participate in over $5 billion in real estate transactions, form a diversified international investment firm, and then have the opportunity to write about it with the hope that others might benefit? Dreams do come true. Just keep your eyes on the timing.

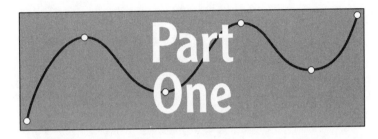

Part One

Why Timing the Market Is the Best Way to Make Money in Real Estate

Timing, Timing, Timing!

I n my early years of real estate investing, I was guided by myriad "how to" books. Among my favorite authors was William Nickerson, who wrote *I Turned $1,000 into a Million in Real Estate in My Spare Time*. Then there was the autobiography of William Zeckendorf.

I now realize that for all their helpful advice, books on real estate investing have historically missed the mark when it comes to the critical issue of timing. Timing is often the single most important factor determining the success or failure of a real estate transaction.

How do I know this? Over a 35-year career in real estate investing, I have bought, sold, managed, and developed hundreds of properties worth a total of over $5 billion. I have owned every type of real estate, from single-family houses to office parks to hotels to 1,000-unit apartment complexes, even Napa Valley vineyards. I have watched decades of real estate cycles come and go, creating great wealth for me and my investors at their peaks and, in a few dark valleys, bringing me to the point of bankruptcy. Over the years I have learned—the hard way—some extremely valuable principles for maximizing investment profits in boom times, while minimizing exposure to losses when markets inevitably come down. This book explains the strategies I've learned for successfully buying low and selling high in real estate.

There are three fundamental reasons why the timing of real estate transactions is critical to long-term investment returns:

1. Though most people believe that real estate prices and cash flows are stable, over the long term, this is not true. Instead, most real estate operations and prices are highly cyclical.

2. For most real estate investors, cash flow is ultimately an insignificant part of overall investment return. Cash flow is rarely as dependable as investors' projections suggest. (More on this in Chapter 2.)

3. If it is true that real estate cash flow and prices are highly cyclical and that cash flow is relatively unimportant to your overall investment return, then by far the two most critical decisions investors will ever need to make are timing when to buy and when to sell.

Timing the Critical Buying Decision

There are two basic approaches to successfully timing real estate purchases. You can be a *momentum* buyer or a *contrarian* buyer. There are pros and cons to each. Provided you are thoughtful about your overall exit strategy, you should be able to make money either way with proper timing. If you're thinking like a trader and have considered how long you plan to own the property, then you should consider what the market will be like when you plan to sell. Will it be a better time then than it is now? And is now the best time to be a buyer?

Momentum and contrarian buyers buy at different times in the cycles.

Timing, Timing, Timing!

Contrarian buyers buy at low points and as close to the bottom as possible, when everyone else is selling. Like me, they buy when there is blood in the streets. This approach is discussed in Chapter 9. The problem with this strategy is that you never really know until after the fact how close you actually made it to the bottom. If you think it's the bottom but the worst is still yet to come, you can get hurt financially unless you have significant staying power. Contrarian buying has the potential to be extremely profitable—but it also can be extremely treacherous.

Momentum buyers, on the other hand, buy once the bottom has been identified and a cycle has started to move up. This approach is discussed in Chapter 10. The problem with this strategy is that you aren't the only one who knows prices are going up. You have to face competition to buy and, under these circumstances, it's difficult not to overpay. You must also be ready to sell relatively quickly, so you don't get caught by a market downturn. To complicate matters further, whether buying or selling, real estate transactions take a long time to complete. Momentum buyers must be careful to time their purchases for the earliest stages of an up cycle.

Whether you are a momentum or a contrarian buyer, you likely won't make money on the cash flow of your investment.... The time to make money is when you sell.

Being prepared, being aware of market cycles, and thinking like a trader before you buy any property—even if you plan to hold onto it for a number of years—is the path to real estate success. Whether you are a momentum or a contrarian buyer, you likely won't make money on the cash flow of your investment during the time that you own it. The time to make money is when you sell.

Throughout my investing history, I have seen some of my own properties go from a positive cash position to a negative one quickly. Because the cyclical nature of real estate dramatically and frequently impacts your bottom-line cash level, it's important to keep a watchful eye on the seven major trends that impact real estate cycles. The foundation of this book is the chapters in Part Two that explain these seven trends and how they interact to create real estate cycles. If you understand how these seven trends are likely to affect the value of real estate in your market over the coming years, you can significantly increase your chances of buying low and selling high.

Timing the Critical Selling Decision

I stumbled into becoming a seller. For many people like me, it has never been easy to let go of real estate. It is easy to get emotionally attached. It also can be fun to see how many properties you can own and control at one time. Selling may be the most difficult part of the equation, but experience has taught me that you need an exit strategy (including a plan for selling at the peak of a real estate cycle) before you buy any property.

Experience has taught me that you need an exit strategy ... before you buy any property.

This exit strategy rarely plays out the way you initially plan. You must have a sell strategy and a plan for managing and improving your property. Today I never make an investment based on cash flow alone. I invest with a plan to add value, enhance the asset physically and otherwise, and ultimately realize profit by selling at the right time in the cycle. Strategizing when you buy about how long you plan to own the property is the beginning of the process of learning about timing.

My First Lesson in Timing the Real Estate Market

On October 10, 1968, I became the proud owner of 427 Hamilton Place. I bought the rooming house in Ann Arbor, Michigan, for $27,250, using

$4,000 in accumulated savings for the down payment. The seller—motivated by the desire to get out of the business—was willing to finance the balance at 7%. This turned out to be quite convenient, because I was too young to actually borrow money from a bank.

Among the many things I didn't know back then was how the lessons learned from this investment would serve me throughout my career. At the time I was pretty certain my involvement in real estate was only a temporary thing. I had no lifelong dream to be in business at all, much less the real estate business. No one in my family was involved in real estate beyond owning a home. My mother was a junior high school art teacher and my father worked in marketing for a camera company.

As it turned out, all of my projections for 427 Hamilton Place were wrong. A tenant on the first floor and basement had a lease at a lower rate than the seller told me. This led to a lawsuit and despite "success" in the lawsuit, between legal fees and higher than expected maintenance costs, I lost money on a cash basis during my ownership. A couple of times I fell behind on payments and almost lost the property to foreclosure. During most of the five years I owned 427 Hamilton Place, I felt like a huge failure as a real estate investor.

But by accident it turned out that I had bought the property when rooming houses and university rental properties were out of fashion—it was a down time in the real estate cycle. When I sold, as luck would have it, the market cycle was at a high point. I sold 427 Hamilton Place for $49,000. Even though I did not receive all cash at closing, over time it was a great return. This was my first lesson in contrarian investing—a lucky stumble into buying low and selling high.

Timing vs. Location

As a young entrepreneur in the real estate business, I heard countless times that what matters most is location, location, location. I don't dispute the validity of this mantra, but location in and of itself cannot protect an investor from buying at the top of a cycle and taking a loss on the way down. Likewise, many consider real estate to be a steady and stable investment with only limited downside potential. If you read about the real estate cycles I've been through and the lessons learned in Chapter 3, you'll see why I think this belief is "absolute hogwash."

A big part of why I bought 427 Hamilton Place was its location. The student tenants could literally roll out of bed and be in class in less than 10 minutes. The building was as close to campus as possible. Despite its great location, as you'll soon see, my $49,000 buyer would have been better served to focus more on timing and location than simply on location alone.

Timing and location are not mutually exclusive. Instead, they naturally complement each other. These two elements are key to all real estate decisions and must work hand in hand. A well-located property purchased when prices are down and at the appropriate time in real estate and economic cycles creates what is called a "barrier to entry" for competition. This is where you want to be. It means that your competition will have trouble building a similar product to compete with yours at the price level of your investment. Both timing and location can create these important barriers to entry, as well as reduce your risk and enhance the return on your investment.

Timing vs. Improving Value

An important strategy I originally learned from one of the many real estate investing books I read early in my career involved making each one of my properties better. I strongly believe that improving the value of an existing property physically, through sound management, enthusiastic marketing, and/or financial restructuring are all-important elements for success.

But improving properties and adding value, just like picking great locations, can fail without good timing. In Chapter 11 I talk about ways to improve your property while you hold it. This can be accomplished as part of a timing-based investment strategy. The combination of superior location and property enhancements are excellent strategies, but only when combined with the essential element of timing.

Why Most Investors Don't Pay Enough Attention to Timing

For years I have seen people set the selling (or buying) price for a property by taking the current cash flow and projecting an inflation rate increase in rents, expenses, and net income on a straight upward moving basis. This simple approach, more often than not, is absolutely wrong.

It ignores the reality of real estate cycles. Because real estate prices are not quoted daily in a marketplace like stocks or bonds, price fluctuations are not obvious. This is why real estate prices and cash flows are often (wrongly) perceived as relatively stable. The reality is that real estate values change dramatically over time.

Unfortunately for the $49,000 buyer of 427 Hamilton Place, he ignored timing. Right after he bought the property from me, the real estate cycle turned downward. I gave him concessions and extra time to make payments, but after two and a half years, he gave up and lost all his investment when he deeded the property back to me. A little over two years after that, I resold 427 Hamilton Place for $52,000, and this time collected all the payments. I began to realize why investors should pay attention to real estate cycles and timing.

To properly time real estate markets, you need to understand what a real estate cycle is and what impacts the cycles.

So, What Is a Real Estate Cycle?

When I refer to a "real estate cycle," I am talking about the movement in property prices from one low point up to the next high point and then back down to the next low point. Typically, there is a plateau period, although sometimes brief, at the top and bottom of each

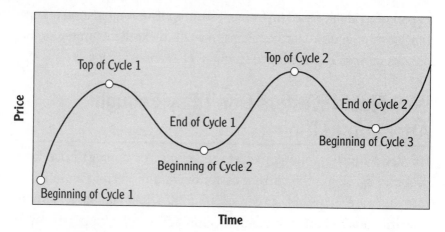

Figure 1-1. Two complete consecutive cycles in the real estate market

cycle. Figure 1-1 shows what two complete consecutive cycles might look like.

Cycles can vary in length of time substantially from one low point to the next. They can be as short as two or three years or as long as eight to 10 years. Within each cycle, real estate prices fluctuate constantly. But because we don't have the benefit of real-time market data and because there are far fewer transactions in real estate than in the stock market, these fluctuations are more difficult to quantify. Even the process of obtaining certified appraisals to determine fair market property prices can take 30 days or more to complete. And those are still just educated opinions, not real prices. Gathering factual data on prices can be time-consuming and tedious and you must think of those prices in ranges, as opposed to absolute numbers.

A typical real estate cycle lasting five years or so may involve prices going up anywhere from 30% to 60% before peaking and beginning a downward move. Downward moves have historically been less pronounced, with percentage changes before the next upturn ranging from 10% to 40%. Over the long term, real estate prices move much the same way as stock prices. Just as stock prices as a whole go up due to increases in earnings per share, real estate prices tend to go up based on increases in property operating income.

Over time, inflation causes rent, operating income, and prices to go up. The key, though, is that they do not go up in a straight line, but fluctuate significantly along the way.

Maximizing Your Returns Through Timing

If you apply timing strategies to your real estate investments, you will, over the long run, enjoy greater profitability and safety. Of course everyone thinks about timing somewhat when they invest in real estate. The difference for most investors is that this is merely a secondary thought. Often a real estate investment may be an emotional purchase at a time when everyone is feeling good about the real estate market. In that circumstance, a typical real estate investor buys near the top of a market, thinking the upward trend in prices is going to continue endlessly, not realizing that it is really near a turning point where things are about to turn downward.

In Figure 1-2, the investor bought a property for $140,000 in year five of a real estate cycle. He then held the property and rode the pric-

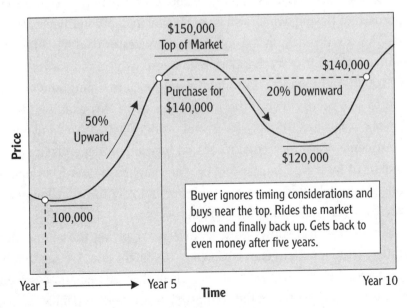

Figure 1-2. Typical real estate investments without applying timing strategy

11

ing up for a short time and then downward for a few years. If we were able to track the daily property price fluctuations like we can do with stocks, it might have taken five years for this investment to get back to its original $140,000 price level. Assuming the investor holds the property for seven, eight, or nine years, he likely would sell it for a profit. With mortgage debt and leverage, the profit might even result in a favorable return of 15% or more per year.

So what is wrong with this picture?

The problem is, this typical real estate investor has taken on more risk than he needed to and suffered more along the way than he needed to. Because he wasn't thinking about timing, he bought too late in the cycle. Had he been more thoughtful, he probably would have realized it wasn't the right time to buy. Or at least he would have made sure he was financially prepared to ride out a downward trend in prices as well as cash flow from the property. While staying power and time generally cure paying too much in the beginning, they also increase the risk and lower the return.

On the other hand, as Figure 1-3 shows, if we apply the contrarian approach to buying, which will be explained in depth in Chapter 9, we may buy a little early. In this example, the investor paid $105,000 for an investment property that bottomed out in value almost a year later at $100,000. If she takes a thoughtful approach to timing, she may be able to sell shortly before the market peaks. In this example, we're showing a sale at $145,000, for a total profit of $40,000 on a five-year investment. While the actual return on investment depends upon the amount of mortgage on the property and any cash flow from operations, ultimately this contrarian investor is likely to be making well over 20% per year on her investment.

Figure 1-3 also shows how an investor applying the momentum strategy (explained in detail in Chapter 10) might fare. We see that he purchased the property once it was clear that property prices were increasing—one year after the contrarian investor—and paid $120,000 for it. Usually the first significant increase in property prices in a cycle

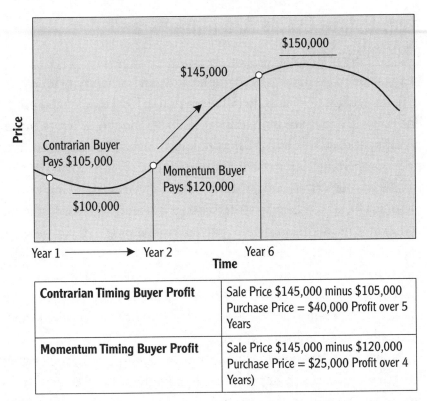

Figure 1-3. Typical real estate investments when applying contrarian or momentum strategies

occurs rapidly, before momentum buyers can get in on it, but the momentum investor believes the trend is just beginning. The momentum investor in Figure 1-3 applies the same timing skills for selling as the contrarian investor and sells the property in year six at $145,000. In this case the momentum investor has a profit of $25,000 (the difference between the $145,000 sale price and the $120,000 purchase price).

All other things being equal, the momentum investor will make a lower return than the contrarian investor. In theory, the momentum investor is taking less risk because the upward cycle has clearly started. On the other hand, contrarian investors like me would argue that the lower the price versus the intrinsic value of the property, the greater the margin of safety. Of course investors can make money with both strategies

Real Estate Cycles Are Market- and Property-Specific

Real estate cycles differ by geographic area and property type. While national real estate trends do influence prices, local market and property-specific cycles are more critical to understanding when to make investment decisions. It can't hurt to know in general that real estate prices are going up in the Southwest and going down in the Northeast, but within each of these regional cycles, there are multiple other local trends at work (discussed in Part Two). For instance, if you are considering purchasing an apartment property, you need to look at cyclical data specific to apartment properties. And if you are interested in hotels, you need to review hotel data, and so on.

The seven major trends, described in Part Two, affect each local market in different ways. These trends can help you predict future price movement or justify past changes.

In the early 1980s, for example, the Southwest experienced rapid job growth as a result of increased in-migration. Even though new construction was plentiful, there was not enough new supply. In fact, three of the seven major trends—job growth, in-migration, and new construction—were each in their own way strongly pushing prices up. At the same time in the Midwest, two of these same trends were causing price movement in exactly the opposite direction. Job loss and out-migration resulted in weakened demand and caused prices to go down in the Midwest.

My company had apartment properties in both regions at that time. Figure 1-4 shows a general representation of what was happening to prices of apartments. Although they were similar assets, our apartment properties in the Southwest were increasing in value while those in the Midwest saw their prices declining. The point is that, although there are national real estate cycles, certain asset types can be moving in opposite directions during the same national real estate cycle.

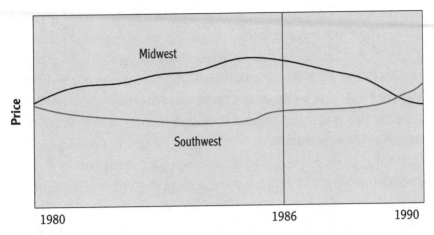

Figure 1-4. Generalized view of regional cycles

Seven Major Trends Impacting Real Estate Cycles

When it comes to timing, there is much to be said for intuition and luck. But relying on luck without knowledge and skill is risky business. Understanding how to evaluate the impact of critical factors on real estate timing cycles can help you develop your gut instincts about timing and improve your chances of success.

When it comes to timing, there is much to be said for intuition and luck. But relying on luck without knowledge and skill is risky business.

I have identified seven major national and local economic trends that directly or indirectly impact real estate cycles, prices, and cash flow:

1. Inflation
2. Interest rates
3. Flow of funds into real estate
4. Job growth
5. In- or out-migration
6. Path of progress
7. New construction

For example, job growth may go in one direction for a period of time, stop, and then reverse. Job growth in any given market is a major trend that affects the demand for many types of real estate.

This book is based on an analysis of how the seven trends come together to create a real estate cycle. They are each individually significant, but they must be studied together. Four of the seven major economic trends directly influence real estate profitability or "net operating income," and you should consider them carefully when planning to buy. The other three trends tend to have a more important impact on capitalization rates (cap rates). Net operating income and cap rates are defined and their impact on property pricing and timing are discussed in Chapter 4. How these trends interact with each other helps us judge when to buy, when to hold, and when to sell any given piece of real estate.

Sources of Timing Cycles

During good times, job growth, local market in-migration, and a favorable national economy with desirable interest and inflation rates all lead to higher demand for real estate. This demand has two basic flavors: consumer demand (e.g., renters and homebuyers) and investor demand (i.e., real estate buyers). Whether due to consumer demand, investor demand, or both, real estate demand overall rises during good times. Consumer demand can cause rents to go up, contributing to a rise in real estate prices. Likewise, money flowing into real estate investments because the stock market has tanked will cause price increases. This is what then drives a major upward cycle.

Upward cycles of compounding good news can go on for varying periods of time, but they never go on forever. Whether a cycle is a short couple of years or a decade long, the reality is that within every cycle is a period of excess where the need to satisfy the demand side is overcompensated by new supply. For example, in any given market, if there is a need for 1,000 new apartments, it is not uncommon for 30 developers to build 100 new apartments each. Suddenly 3,000 new apartments materialize, which is 2,000 too many. This is the inexact nature of the real estate market. Supply rarely meets demand precisely. Extended upward cycles can be like rubber bands—the longer and stronger they are pulled in one direction, the more they shoot in the opposite direction. In other words, a terrific boom is most likely to be followed by a terrific bust.

Because real estate is a tangible, physical asset, it seems to provide a degree of safety and comfort to investors. But appearances can be deceiving. Within each cycle, great amounts of wealth can be made—and lost. Understanding the nature of the booms and the busts, including the associated cyclical trends, should help protect you from potential disasters as well as improve your chances of higher returns.

Successful Timing Can Be Learned

When I have been interviewed about my real estate transactions that were well timed, I have used words like "fortunate" and "luck." It is my firm view that luck does indeed play a role in success. But timing is more important. In a sense, you can learn to put your investments in the position to be "lucky."

This book is devoted to explaining the seven trends that drive real estate cycles and how understanding these trends can help you predict the direction of the next real estate cycle. Armed with a sense of market timing, you can routinely be buying at or near the bottom of real estate cycles and selling at or near the top of real estate cycles. Learning to sense the opportunities and pitfalls in the market will greatly improve your odds for success as a real estate investor.

The Myth of Cash Flow:
Why You Don't Make Money
"Owning" Real Estate

Many investors and even so-called experts think of real estate investment returns as being in great part from cash flow. Projections of 8% to 10% or even greater cash flow returns are often considered as a key part of a hoped for ultimate 15% to 20% annual return. But, as I briefly stated at the beginning of the book, and as this chapter will further demonstrate, for most real estate the reality is very different. Of course there are properties with very low mortgages that produce dependable cash flow, but for my analysis we're talking about investment properties with typical maximum debt levels.

As this chapter will show, the reality is that cash flow should be looked at as a minor part of your return rather than half or more of your return, as traditional real estate investment theory has suggested. The reason this is so important is that, if I am correct about the points in this chapter on why you can't count on cash flow, then the timing of when you buy and sell becomes all the more critical.

Cash flow is affected by many factors, but especially by leverage. Because real estate usually is bought and sold with maximum mortgage levels, the net cash flow is small relative to the gross income and expenses. This means relatively small changes to income and expense can have a large impact on cash flow. Cash flow can disappear virtually overnight in a down real estate market or even in isolated situations, such as losing your tenant on a rental house and having difficulty replacing that tenant.

Having expenses greater than income on a property is called "negative cash flow." This means that you are paying the difference out of your own pocket. I have had experience with negative cash flow more times than I care to recall. If you own a real estate investment that experiences negative cash flow, you will begin to wonder why so many experts tell you to hold real estate for the long term. You may also wonder if your problems are unique. The truth is you are not the first one to experience negative cash flow. One of the main causes of negative cash flow is the fact that real estate investors consistently underestimate the amount of money they will need to pay out over the long term for capital improvements to their properties. When I started my real estate investing career, I was no different.

My First Big Lesson About How Real Estate Is Not a Cash Flow Business

In 1969 I developed a system for raising money from investors (beginning with my fellow college students) that allowed me to purchase about 20 properties over the period of just a few years. The time burdens of managing all those properties while taking college courses eventually became too much to handle—and I dropped out of school to become a full-time real estate investor.

But soon the bills started to pile up and I wasn't able to pay them. My accounting system for all 20 properties consisted of placing the bills as they arrived in an old cigar box and then taking them out one by one when I felt I had collected enough rent money to write checks. Between vacuuming floors, pretending to be a plumber, and dodging the student tenant union picketers (who had targeted me just because I was known to be a successful landlord), I knew it was time to face the money music. I took a deep breath, pulled out the box, and totaled up all the bills. I had to pick myself up off the floor when I realized I had $10,832 in bills I could not pay. I was in desperate financial shape.

My First Lesson in the Importance of Selling

Up to this point, my investors had been patient, but the promised returns weren't materializing. My projections had clearly shown that I would pay them back out of property cash flows. Had I known then the truth about capital expenditures and the fact that cash flows were likely to be nonexistent, I would have told them so—and no one would have invested with me. Then there would have been no buildings and I wouldn't have been in this predicament. It was a Catch-22 situation.

Demoralized, I began making plans to sell.

What transpired next was for me a true timing revelation. It became clear that when I had started buying real estate I was buying at the bottom of a cycle during a tumultuous time. Now, three years later, the market had calmed down. The tenant union rent strikes had failed year after year and were being abandoned. Property values were up, as was the demand for student housing. Investors seemed to come from anywhere and everywhere looking to get into the business.

With the help of some smart brokers, I learned the advantages of offering financing to the buyers of my buildings. Over the next several months, I used this method to sell and finance every one of my student properties. Even though all my profit was tied up in the value of the mortgages I was now holding, I was able to get a much higher price for the buildings than if I had sold them outright for cash, because financing from banks was hard to get. Out of the down payments, I paid back all my investors right away, plus a portion of the promised returns. Then, over the next several years, I was able to pay them back completely—not only the returns they had missed, but also additional significant gains on their original investments.

I had become a paper millionaire. The key to it all was fortunate timing. I could just as easily have been unlucky. ... I eventually learned to reduce (though not eliminate) the luck factor.

In just a little over three years and before the age of 21, I felt as though I had survived until the timing was right. Somehow I had turned my $4,000 life savings into $1 million in net equity. I had become a paper millionaire. The key to it all was fortunate timing. I could just as easily have been unlucky. Later chapters in the book will show you how I eventually learned to reduce (though not eliminate) the luck factor when timing my real estate purchases and sales.

The Greatest Lie in Real Estate

One of the reasons cash flow often ends up being less than investors project is that capital expenditures (for new roofs, boilers, plumbing, etc.) are consistently higher than anyone expects them to be. Keep in mind this simple truth: "Things never work out quite the way they are planned." And also keep in mind this greatest lie in real estate: "It will only take $XX to cover needed real estate improvements on this property."

Every single one of the first 20 buildings I bought was represented to be in great shape, needing only minor repairs, if any at all. It was only after the inspections were over and closings were completed that all the hidden problems began to show up. In the beginning, I thought my miscalculations in this area were due to my own lack of experience. But as time passed, I found that it honestly costs much more to run a property than you ever think it could.

I didn't take into consideration the need for new appliances or paint or replacing carpeting or siding. I didn't factor in recurring non-operating expenses either, or plan for unexpected vacancies or turnover. What I have learned since then is that capital expenditures (such as replacing a leaky roof) are truly critical day-to-day needs and should be accounted for as such. If you defer maintenance by not taking care of problems as they occur, your properties will deteriorate faster and faster. You'll end up having to reduce the rent. Your ability to attract quality residents will decline. In the end, you'll be caught in a downward spiral.

Keep in mind this greatest lie in real estate: "It will only take $XX to cover needed real estate improvements on this property."

So, when you hear "It will only take $XX to cover needed real estate improvements on this property" or similar statements, you must recognize the greatest lie in real estate. It's one that's told over and over by even the best-intentioned lenders, brokers, and sellers. In fact, it actually seems to have become an unspoken rule that this lie must be perpetuated. How else could you explain it?

It actually seems to have become an unspoken rule that this lie must be perpetuated. How else could you explain it?

You also might wonder why the financial statements for the property don't reflect these capital expense requirements. It seems logical enough, and I used to try to detect these requirements in the financial statements for properties I was looking at purchasing. You'll sometimes find that the seller spent a lot of money several years ago "catching up on a neglected property" to get it ready to sell. But more typically you'll be shown only the expenses for the year prior to the sale, which will be artificially low. You'll be encouraged to believe these numbers represent normal expenditures, but they don't. Or you may enjoy hearing strange and extraordinary stories about why the property experienced a "temporary period of higher expenses" and all the many reasons why you should never again expect to spend that much. Contrary to all that, no matter the property's location, type, or size, capital expenditures are a vital link to understanding true cash flow and real value.

It is my belief that properties need to be maintained at a fairly high level on a regular basis. Whether a small rooming house, a single-family rental property, or a huge office complex, never underestimate the actual cost of capital reserves you will need in order to afford to pay for that new roof as soon as you need it. If you use realistic numbers to calculate a prospective property's cash flow and remember that sellers and agents are playing a capital expenditures game with you, you'll be better prepared to play and win.

The Second Greatest Lie in Real Estate

Lucky timing saved me from my first financial crisis as a real estate investor. But you can't count on luck. However, you can count on the fact that your expenses and capital expenditures will, over time, eat up most or all of your positive cash flow. Perhaps a little more attention to my accounting class would have helped me make better cash flow projections on my first properties. I might have seen more quickly that reality was far from "budget" and "projection." How could every single one of my properties require more money than I was receiving in rent? I began to try to analyze exactly what had happened—and the second greatest lie in real estate started to become very clear.

"Real estate is a cash flow business." There it is—the second greatest lie in real estate. If real estate were the cash machine it's represented to be, where was all that money going? If you defer maintenance, you begin a downward spiral that ultimately will damage your property's long-term value. If you spend money on maintenance, and I firmly believe you must, your expenses come right out of anticipated cash flow. The second greatest lie in real estate is tied directly to the first. And the truth shall set you free.

"Real estate is a cash flow business." There it is—the second greatest lie in real estate.

If real estate isn't a cash flow business, then why are so many people in it for that? The reality is, money can be made from property operations, but the real money is made when you sell. To help illustrate why real estate isn't a consistent cash flow business, it is helpful to understand the components that make up cash flow:

	$Revenues
Less	– Operating Expenses
Equals	Net Operating Income (NOI)
Less	– Capital Expenses
Less	– Mortgage Payments
Equals	$Net Cash Flow

Each of these components (revenues, operating expenses, capital expenses, and mortgage payments) can and do fluctuate based on numerous factors, making net cash flow all the more unpredictable.

REVENUES

The vast majority of property revenues come from rent paid by tenants; however, there are additional sources of revenue that vary by property type. In hotels, for example, additional income can be generated by restaurants, bars, catering services, gift shop proceeds, etc. Likewise, apartment properties earn additional income through laundry fees, parking charges, furniture rentals, and so on.

Revenues can be driven by a number of supply-and-demand factors and can and will fluctuate as a result. Revenues drop quickly and dramatically during a real estate downturn.

Operating Expenses

Operating expenses generally include all day-to-day costs associated with running the property, such as insurance, utilities, staff payroll, taxes, cleaning supplies, etc. These hard costs are highly influenced by external trends, including inflation, commodity prices, and overall supply and demand, varying by specific market area. They can and frequently do actually increase during a real estate downturn.

One example is apartments. During a downturn, you will generally have more move-outs. Vacant apartments must be cleaned, repaired, and prepared for new tenants. The higher volume of move-outs increases this expense.

Capital Expenses

Capital expenses are the costs associated with significant physical purchases or improvements to the property with normal life expectancies of five or more years, such as a new roof, new air conditioning system, or repaved concrete driveway. These expenses often are underestimated and misrepresented by a seller to the extent that cash flow projections and plans are thrown way off course.

The interpretation of what is a capital expense and what is not varies from person to person. For example, if one takes the position that routine replacement of carpeting is a capital expense, property NOI can appear unrealistic and artificially inflated because these expenses are not deducted from NOI. It is important to consider capital expenses with a realistic cost of operations. Most buyers significantly underestimate capital expenditures.

Mortgage Payments

Mortgage payments constitute the regular monthly or quarterly payments of principal and interest to the mortgage lender, often referred to as "debt service." The pros and cons of mortgages and their impact on your investment return are addressed further in Chapter 8. In short, the structure of a mortgage has a great impact on the variability of your mortgage payment. Some mortgages are based on floating interest rates that change at specified intervals, typically quarterly or annually. These floating rate mortgages can create additional fluctuations in net cash flow. As interest rates change, refinancing to obtain fixed rates may make good sense as a way to improve net cash flow.

Don't Believe the Two Greatest Lies in Real Estate—Instead Concentrate on Timing

If you accept that capital improvements will always be more than you expect and that real estate is not the consistent cash flow machine that so many try to convince you it is, this will free you to think like a trader. You will be able to buy at the low point in cycles and sell at the high point while others suffer through holding their properties during down cycles.

In Chapter 3, I will explain what the major real estate down cycles have been in my 35 years in the real estate business, how you can learn from them, and how history can help you predict future cycles.

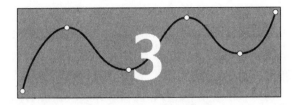

Lessons I've Learned from Real Estate Cycles of the Last 35 Years

I f someone had told me 35 years ago about the uniqueness of each real estate cycle and the impact of the seven major trends on pricing (to be explained in Chapter 5), I'm pretty sure I would have listened. The reality is that, throughout my 35-year investment career, I learned about the cycles and the seven trends the hard way. Things that may seem obvious or simple now are often difficult to understand in the middle of a storm. I hope that sharing my experiences with you will help you capitalize on the up side and avoid the down side of real estate investing.

1974–1976: Big Opportunity in a Down Market

It's not uncommon for one or two trends to dominate a cycle. In Michigan during the mid-1970s, the apartment cycle was dominated by negative job growth and out-migration trends. The auto industry in Michigan had imploded. Unemployment had risen dramatically in

1974 and 1975. With these job losses came one-way U-Haul rentals and a mass exodus to parts of the country with healthier economies. At the time, with oil prices rising, Texas and other Southwestern markets were booming.

Most of the United States, in fact, was in an economic slump. The Dow Jones Industrial stock market index had gone from approximately 1,000 in late 1973 to less than 700 in early 1975. Prices for most types of real estate in many parts of the country were down, but because of its dependence on the auto industry, Michigan and the Midwest were the hardest hit. Texas properties were among the few that were not only holding their own but also actually going up in value, boosted by high oil and gas prices.

In Michigan, from 1974 to 1976, real estate prices were falling. To survive in the real estate and property management business, I worked feverishly seven days a week at a pace some friends used to say would kill me before I turned 30. But the timing was right to buy and I was focused on taking advantage of great purchase opportunities.

In the spring of 1974, after months of negotiation, we purchased the Woodcrest Villas apartment complex in Westland, Michigan, a suburb of Detroit. Throughout the negotiation process, the property's occupancy level had continued to drop. In fact, occupancies were going down throughout the entire suburban Detroit submarket. Even back then, our company's strategy included an ownership plan that spanned a number of years, designed to outlast a cyclical down market. The fact that occupancy had declined at Woodcrest to the mid-70% level by the time we closed seemed to us like nothing more than a minor challenge.

Woodcrest Villas was enormous, with a total of 432 units and a 10,000-square-foot clubhouse. It also had a huge heated indoor/outdoor pool that to me at the time was the most exciting thing I could imagine. I remember one December day swimming from the indoor portion of the pool, under the glass divider, outside to where the snow was gently falling. It was exhilarating and a memory that to this day gives me a tremendous feeling of pride and pleasure.

Somewhat to my surprise, the purchase of Woodcrest Villas was followed by bigger and even more exciting opportunities. Next we bought an even larger apartment property named Knob on the Lake. Then we made a large land purchase in Longboat Key, Florida, followed by even more apartment acquisitions in Michigan.

The limited partnerships we were assembling became bigger and bigger to accommodate our growth and the cash requirements of the larger assets. Throughout the mid-1970s, we continued buying, believing that the cycle was at its low point. Later we learned we had bought a little early. Had we waited, we most likely would have been able to buy at even lower prices and would have avoided some of the cash flow difficulties ahead.

Real estate prices remained low for a number of years even after the worst of our national recession had passed. Michigan's economy slowly recovered and we saw again that the time to be aggressive is at the lowest point of a cycle. While we had become somewhat knowledgeable about surviving difficult times, this particular time period turned out to be longer and harder to endure than we had thought.

We saw again that the time to be aggressive is at the lowest point of a cycle.

When times got better, we sold a number of properties purchased in the mid-1970s, producing annualized returns of 25% to 150%. Luckily, we had a happy and supportive investor base that patiently waited for the returns to come. Often it seemed we survived and prospered by sheer willpower alone. Our investors survived and prospered right along with us.

LESSONS LEARNED AND PRACTICAL TIPS

Real estate is indeed cyclical! Certain economic trends, such as employment levels, help us understand the timing of these cycles. Contrary to the perception that real estate is a steady investment less volatile than stocks, most real estate is in fact highly cyclical. Learning to understand the causes of economic and other trends affecting cycles can teach you how to take advantage of opportunities and avoid unnecessary risks. *An economic and real estate slump is often the best time to buy!*

While others are afraid to invest in real estate, you can benefit from lower prices and greater availability of prime properties. Take advantage of the downsides of cycles.

1981-1982: Opportunities in a Down Market in the Southwest

By 1981, we had expanded into surrounding states and into the Southwest. Again, we found ourselves in a national economic recession similar to the 1974-to-1976 period, although not as bad. This recession negatively impacted new job creation and in some markets caused job losses—one of the worst things that can happen to a real estate market. Our prior successes at buying through the downturn bolstered our confidence and our investors' confidence in us. We bought aggressively at lower prices than ever before and once again found the downward part of the cycle to be our time of greatest opportunity.

> We bought aggressively at lower prices than ever before and once again found the downward part of the cycle to be our time of greatest opportunity.

It was during this time in the Southwest in 1981 that we encountered a new trend—too much new construction. Job losses resulted in reduced demand for apartments, but optimistic developers continued to build. Luckily, by 1983, the national economy recovered and almost at once all of the excess apartments were leased. As we were to learn, the Southwest was a far more volatile market than the

Midwest. At one moment it would appear that there was far too much new construction, and then at the next moment, due to in-migration and job growth, the supply would be absorbed. This proved to be true for all commercial property types: multifamily, retail, and office.

Then we learned about another trend that affects real estate market timing, called "flow of funds." This trend created huge growth for us—and nearly sent us into bankruptcy when it ended.

Another trend ..., called "flow of funds," ... created huge growth for us—and nearly sent us into bankruptcy when it ended.

In response to a concern about the economic downturn and a general reluctance by investors to invest in real estate, the Reagan administration had passed The Economic Recovery Tax Act of 1981. The Act created multiple incentives for real estate investors, including shortened depreciation of 15 years. It caused a tremendous boom in the real estate market. Suddenly my company was growing by leaps and bounds, driven by investors who wanted to take advantage of the tax benefits. We were certain we were doing the right thing by getting bigger. We believed in the government's programs and enjoyed the new tax benefits those programs introduced. We also expected the economy to pick up so that properties we were investing in would be met with higher demand.

We were hooked. More to the point, our investors were hooked. The new tax laws were designed to provide investors with tax savings each year at least equal to their original investments—an incredibly good deal. Some investors were in tax brackets as high as 70% and the tax benefits gave them immediate relief. We found ourselves opening multi-million dollar investment offerings (called "syndications") on Friday afternoons, only to be sold out before the following Monday morning. We simply could not buy apartments fast enough to fuel this syndication machine.

My company, Hall Financial Group, was named the largest real estate private placement sponsor in the United States—having raised more than $320 million in 1985 alone. All told, as of 1985, we had raised and invested over $1 billion in equity. About three-fourths of that occurred in the four years from 1981 to 1985, and we were expanding feverishly, driven by the momentum. Instead of buying in down periods like we had done in 1974 to 1976 and 1981 to 1982, by 1983 we were buying in a market with prices rising and were not being nearly as thoughtful about timing as we had been previously and are today.

LESSONS LEARNED AND PRACTICAL TIPS

All real estate cycles are local! Although national economic trends influence real estate markets, each local market reacts differently. You need to be extremely local-market-specific as you analyze timing and consider the cycles.

Government policies can be leading indicators of major trend changes that will affect real estate timing! As you will learn in Chapter 5, there are seven major real estate trends, three of which are national in scope. In various cycles, capital flows—one of the national trends—can be highly influenced by government policy. If, as in the case of the 1981 Tax Act, you see a government policy that in time will dramatically increase the amount of money going into real estate, you can buy ahead of the impact of the trend changes and reap substantial benefits.

1986–1990: Success Made Us Forget About Timing the Market—and We Ended in Disaster

Too much success too quickly can be blinding and the bumps in the road—if you feel them at all—appear justifiable and temporary. It was in this giddy atmosphere that my workday began on December 10, 1985. Though the day began normally, it wouldn't end that way.

I had just completed a stock transaction that would net a $12 million profit and was feeling pretty good. The holidays were just around the corner, and I was looking forward to spending some time with my family at our Florida condo.

Too much success too quickly can be blinding.

"I was just on my way to see you," said Don Braun, our assistant treasurer, in a somewhat concerned tone. Standing 6'7" tall, Don was, and still is, difficult to ignore. His department had just completed revising the November budgets for the 350 partnerships we controlled.

"Combined," he said, "we are $11 million short at the end of November. And based on December projections, we're going to need a similar amount again before year-end."

Stunned, I had to sit down. Don and I talked about why we hadn't seen this coming. Rental incomes had declined and operating expenses had gone up. Interest payments remained constant. What seemed to us to have been ample cash reserves at one moment turned out to be insufficient the next. The challenges of maneuvering through downturns like this weren't pleasant. But this particular situation would also turn out to be most unusual.

Before it was over, this mid-1980s downturn would become the worst real estate collapse in recent history. In some ways it made the 1930s look tame by comparison. The real problem was to come in 1986 and beyond, as rents and other revenues continued to free-fall with no near-term hope for stabilization.

But on that December day in 1985, we still thought we could figure it all out somehow. And even though we were concerned, we had no earthly idea things were about to get as bad as they did. Don began to summarize his findings. Total annual rent revenues for all our properties combined were running right at $300 million. Even a 5% decline in those revenues could negatively impact our cash flow by $15 million.

The only reasonable action Don and I could come up with was to notify our investors and lenders about what was happening. We felt a responsibility to provide them with accurate and complete information. Most of our company employees spent the remainder of December, including all the Christmas season and New Year's Eve, preparing detailed analyses of every property, including existing and projected operations, mortgage levels, and analysis regarding the ability of each property to make associated mortgage payments. Armed with this information, we notified our lenders and investors of our concerns that the properties might not be able to remain current on mortgage obligations without some modifications to the original mortgage terms. We were optimistic things would be worked out because we were not and had never been in default on any of our obligations.

We rather naively thought that we could contact our lenders and investors, tell them the truth about what was happening, and discuss ways we could all quietly work things out together. We were the first major company to admit to the looming problems—and we couldn't have been more wrong as to how our disclosure would be received. A firestorm of media, virtually all of it negative, followed the correspondence to our lenders and investors. It also angered the competition, still either unaware of or committed to hiding the truth about the market's problems.

We were the first major company to admit to the looming problems—and we couldn't have been more wrong as to how our disclosure would be received.

Thankfully, because of our long track record of forthrightness with our investors, they were extremely supportive. Our lender response, though, was less than positive and certainly not productive. We told them everything we knew and offered to work toward a mutually beneficial resolution that included committing to new investment capital. Without their cooperation, mortgage defaults were inevitable. To our surprise and dismay, our lenders were completely unwilling to discuss any loan modifications. We also quickly found out that many of our lenders were also in trouble and were quietly being run by savings and loan regulators.

Thus began a seven-year odyssey of trying to survive this deep down cycle. Over time we were able to modify many of our partnerships—some with the assistance of lenders and some, unfortunately, through the bankruptcy courts. In the end, we restructured over $1 billion in mortgage debt. We lost a number of properties to foreclosure and our investors experienced some losses, but it could have been much worse. We were not legally required to put funds back into our money-losing properties, except for a small guaranteed amount. But if we did not support the properties with added cash, our investors—who had each contributed from $50,000 to $150,000—would lose everything.

Over the next several years, I liquidated the majority of my personal holdings to loan $175 million to these limited partnerships. In the end, I was forced to regroup after filing personal Chapter 11 bankruptcy.

Lessons Learned and Practical Tips

Do not get carried away with success and forget the basics! In short, do not believe your own press or what your mother or spouse says about how smart you are. Humility is an investor's best friend. This is a game full of plenty of hard work and basic business.

Trend investing does not work forever! Even though it may seem like things will never turn down, you must believe that they will. Good times do not last forever. Be careful to either get out in time or at least have your debt in comfortable shape.

A Review of the "100-Year Flood" of 1986-1990

Obviously it's much easier to see what happened now that it's all behind us. The real estate crash that began in late 1985 had, by 1990, turned into the most serious economic disaster in 100 years.

When people speak of floods, they generally refer to events that occur every 10 years or so. The worst floods are called "100-year floods" because they are the most severe in a century. For our industry, in many parts of the United States, what was happening to the real estate sector specifically in the late 1980s was worse than the Great Depression of the 1930s. We clearly faced a 100-year flood.

This was the absolute worst of times. A quick review sheds some light on this great down cycle and helps us answer the question, "What had happened to us?"

Those of us in Dallas, Texas, where my company was based, were in the epicenter of the storm. To make matters even more difficult for us as large apartment owners, the apartment sector was one of the hardest hit real estate sectors, second only to raw land. Apartment prices fell from their highs in 1985 by 30% and even 60% of their values before the recovery started. The office market was also severely impacted. A number of brand-new office buildings that cost over $150 per square foot to build were eventually sold at government auctions for as little as $25 per square foot. Respected and reputable financial institutions were going broke.

This was the absolute worst of times. A quick review sheds some light on this great down cycle and helps us answer the question, "What had happened to us?"

SUPPLY AND DEMAND WERE WAY OUT OF WHACK

Throughout the early 1980s, real estate supply had dramatically increased. Then, due to the 1986 national economic recession, demand significantly decreased. In Texas, a decline in oil prices reduced the need for all types of real estate even further. Jobs in the energy industry evaporated, forcing many workers to move to other states. In hindsight, we should have known supply was growing too fast. Blinded by the boom of the early 1980s, however, no one examined new construction trends on the radar screen.

ENTER THE U.S. GOVERNMENT

Starting with The Economic Recovery Tax Act of 1981, the government induced funds to flow into real estate. Then, a few years later, it pulled the rug out from under the public with The Tax Reform Act of 1986. The incentives in 1981 created new construction that wasn't needed and existing properties changed hands at higher-than-ever prices even while vacancies rose. Income from operations decreased across the board, yet with so much money chasing the investment opportunities, prices continued to soar. With inflation and interest rates relatively high and growing, many of us justified our ever-increasing optimism about real estate. As we purchased properties, we continued to be overly optimistic in our profit projections.

Late in 1985, the market began to fall of its own weight. At the worst of all possible times, Congress passed the 1986 Tax Reform Act, for the first time in history retroactively punishing investors who had counted on consistent fairness in tax policy. Write-offs for real estate losses, the original incentives introduced in 1981, were now categorized as passive losses with severe limitations as write-offs against ordinary income. This also brought an almost instantaneous halt to the already declining investment capital flow. Between declining NOIs and the halt in the flow of funds, we thought things couldn't get any worse, but in fact, they could—and did.

The ultimate decline in property values that supported mortgages caused not only owners and investors to lose money, but lenders as well. Savings and loans and banks suffered huge losses from foreclosures on real estate, eventually causing a vast number of them to go broke. The banks and savings and loans themselves were ultimately taken over by the federal government. In charge of so many savings and loans and banks, the government regulators created the Federal Asset Disposition Association in 1985 to dispose of the foreclosed assets. This agency was replaced in 1990 by another agency, the Resolution Trust Corporation (RTC).

Instead of creating new mortgages on properties, or at least waiting until the market had stabilized, the RTC took drastic action. Foreclosed real estate was placed on the market to sell for cash only at what turned out to be the lowest point in the market cycle. Doing this was much less complicated from a political standpoint than selling on terms or renegotiating mortgages with the property owners, but far worse in terms of payments received by the government for prime real estate. To the government, these drastic actions seemed less likely to draw criticism. Companies such as General Electric Credit Corporation, the Bass Family, and others made fortunes paying extremely low prices and then holding the properties until prices rose dramatically just a few years later.

In addition to this transfer of wealth, the overall market deflated. In the mid 1980s, U.S. government agencies involved in regulating lending institutions forced these lenders to take huge paper losses related to bad loans. Finally, toward the end of the 198s, the regulators were generating fire sales that could not have come at a worse time. Prices fell much further than they would have without government intervention. These cash-only sales demanded by the RTC resulted in very low prices and created a cloud over the entire United States real estate market.

LESSONS LEARNED AND PRACTICAL TIPS

Although cycles repeat, they are also unique—and it is important to judge the specifics at the time! The 1986 real estate collapse was far worse than most real estate cycles in terms of prices dropping in a short time. But, as you will learn later in this book, you can benefit by acting ahead of the decline, based on the direction and character of the trends that influence real estate cycles.

Historically, cycles have certain dependable aspects and are a part of the real estate investment "laws of nature," as I call them, but when the government intervenes, extremes can be exaggerated! Be mindful and react quickly to any government involvement, directly or indirectly, in real estate markets. Government efforts, no matter how well intended, may cause negative exaggerated deflation, as in the case of the RTC. Alternatively, an expansive Federal Reserve money supply, all other things being equal, will likely result in positive price increases.

1991-1992: Another Down Cycle

After the chaos of 1986 to 1990, things picked up briefly, due in large part to the fact that the real estate business had nowhere to go but up. An influx of Japanese capital was also a big driver. But 1990 brought only a brief uptick in property pricing.

From 1991 to 1992, recession put the brakes on what could have been a material recovery. Luckily, this recession also turned out to be rather brief, and real estate overall didn't suffer a huge hit. Lower interest rates, which kept property prices from dropping too much, made property ownership easier and more beneficial. From the beginning of 1990 to the end of 1992, 30-year fixed-rate mortgages dropped from a high of 10% to a low of 8.4%. This was just the beginning of what would become a long-term decline in interest rates that would bolster real estate for the remainder of the decade.

2000-2003: How Trends Work Against One Another

Hopefully, you have begun to see that every real estate cycle is different. Cycles often have some common trends driving them, but they all vary to a degree. The most interesting factor involved in the down cycle in commercial real estate that began in 2000 is that it was limited because trends were pushing in opposite directions.

To begin with, we had a sluggish economy with significant job losses. The economy was hurt further by the 9/11 tragedy. These factors combined to negatively impact commercial real estate. On the other hand, we had extremely low interest rates, which are good for real estate. Add to this mix vast amounts of money flowing out of the stock market and into real estate beginning in 2001. A good portion of this money sought out real estate as a "safe haven" from the stock market.

Areas most severely impacted by job losses and the loss of tourism saw the largest declines in property prices. Hotels have been hurt the worst, followed by office properties and apartments.

Some markets and property types have been impacted far more severely than others. Areas most severely impacted by job losses and the loss of tourism saw the largest declines in property prices. Hotels have been hurt the worst, followed by office properties and apartments.

While no one could have predicted the events and impact of 9/11, you certainly can learn how to watch the seven major trends and predict how real estate could be impacted by future cycles.

LESSONS LEARNED AND PRACTICAL TIPS

Trends need to be understood individually, but in the real world they work together! Use your knowledge of the individual trends to predict the effect of each individual trend as it interacts with the others. If you understand each one, you have a far greater chance of understanding their combined results and their impact on real estate cycles.

Learning from Past Cycles

Starting with the first major down cycle I experienced in 1974-1976,

Lessons I've Learned from Real Estate Cycles of the Last 35 Years

I became more aware of exactly how cyclical real estate is and I became committed to the process of learning how to take advantage of these cycles in my investment strategy. As noted earlier, in the 1986-1990 downturn, my company failed to pay close enough attention to the signs of an impending downturn and therefore failed to benefit from our hard-earned lessons. Definitely older and slightly wiser today, I try to stay focused on timing issues.

I hope you take from my experience with these cycles an appreciation for timing real estate investments, and that you learn from the remainder of this book how to utilize timing to maximize your returns and minimize your risk.

The Fundamentals of Pricing: Capitalization Rate and Net Operating Income

Timing the real estate markets is really about timing the factors that make property prices go up or down. The price that you can get for your property at any given time will vary significantly depending upon where it stands in the real estate cycle.

Now that you have a general understanding about what a real estate cycle is and realize the need to time your purchase and sale decisions to fit within the cycle, you next need to better understand how properties are priced.

Value vs. Price

The terms "value" and "price" are often used interchangeably. Throughout my discussion of cycles, I will purposefully talk about property *prices* rather than *values*. Value implies the real worth of something. In real estate cycles, prices often go higher and at times lower than what a property's long-term "value" or real worth might be.

The Fundamentals of Pricing

Value can be a bit of an esoteric concept in that it always is based on the views or perspectives of people. Pricing between a knowledgeable buyer and seller without any undue influence at any moment in time basically determines fair market value. However, prices often go to extremes, and intrinsic or "normalized" fair values may be ignored from time to time.

Timing influences prices more than real value. And, at any given moment in time, the price a property can command is far more relevant to investors than what I am calling intrinsic value. But, understating intrinsic value can be beneficial to the timing perspective.

To me, intrinsic value relates back to the basics of cash flow and replacement cost. A good intrinsic value is a price that is significantly below replacement cost.

For example, let's say that you are considering buying a 15-year-old, 2,000-square-foot house as rental property. After doing a little research, you find that this house could be built new for $150,000 and that vacant lots of similar size and quality in the area are going for $30,000. This means the total replacement cost for the house under consideration would be $180,000. Since a new house would have no wear and would include new building materials and the technologies developed over the past 15 years, the rental house should logically sell for less than the replacement amount. However, in an actual demand-driven real estate market, sometimes real estate like this can sell for more than its replacement cost. In this situation, if the rental property was purchased for more than its replacement cost, it would clearly be selling for more than what I believe the real intrinsic value might be.

On the cash flow side, the rental income less expenses and needed capital items should leave a fair current real cash flow. By fair, depending on the time and property details, we might expect a level of from 8% to 10% cash on cash return. But this is often not realistic. Based on these definitions, properties sell for more than their intrinsic value most of the time.

I don't mean you should never purchase a property for more than its intrinsic value. I am saying that it should always be a factor in your decision-making process. It is obviously better when pricing is at real or intrinsic levels, but by the nature of timing cycles that is far from always the case. Understanding intrinsic value is useful, but more useful to your understanding of real estate cycles is to understand the elements that determine actual real estate prices.

> Understanding intrinsic value is useful, but more useful to your understanding of real estate cycles is to understand the elements that determine actual real estate prices.

Determining Prices Throughout Real Estate Cycles

Throughout the remainder of this book, you will learn that there are multiple factors and situations that influence property prices and overall investment returns. I will discuss how pricing typically works in local market scenarios and for specific property types, from both a buyer's and a seller's perspective. I will also give examples and formulas that you can use when planning your strategy.

Before you can truly understand the timing of real estate cycles, you have to understand pricing. There are two key components used to determine real estate prices. The first is *net operating income* (NOI), which refers to the net income a property generates. The second is the *capitalization rate* (cap rate), which refers to the benefits of investing in a particular property relative to investing in other ventures.

Net Operating Income (NOI)

Net operating income (NOI) is defined as revenue less operating expenses prior to debt service (i.e., the mortgage payments) and capital expenditures (e.g., paying for a new roof, etc.).

The Fundamentals of Pricing

In other words, NOI does not equal cash in your pocket, because capital expenditures and mortgage payments have not been deducted. But NOI is important for two reasons. First, dollar for dollar, the higher your NOI, the higher your net cash flow will be: i.e., NOI has a direct impact on cash flow. The second importance of NOI is that it is a part of the basic, common way to compare one property with another. The other component that works hand in hand with NOI is the capitalization rate, which is discussed later.

Net operating income is defined as revenue less operating expenses prior to debt service and capital expenditures.

To calculate a property's NOI, start with its revenue. The revenue sources (other than the obvious one—rents) will vary by property type. In hotels, revenue would include the restaurant, bar, catering, and other retail sales. Apartments may have laundry charges, parking fees, and other revenues. The point is that all income sources are included in total revenue.

Expenses include all day-to-day operating expenses, such as utilities, insurance, or property taxes. A capital expenditure is money spent on a physical item for the property with a life that generally spans at least five years. Things like a new roof or new heating system are obvious capital expenditures. These items are effectively replacing part of the physical asset itself, not paying for day-to-day expenses, and therefore should not be expensed. Instead, these items are treated outside of NOI.

However, there are certain items that fall into a gray area as to whether they should be capital expenditures or not. One such example is carpet replacement. Is this an operating expense or a capital expense? All items that are treated as capital expenditures and not as expenses can potentially inflate NOI by indicating a higher NOI than would be the case if these items were expensed. Therefore, when reviewing a property for potential purchase, evaluate what has been treated as capital items to make sure that you agree with the seller's interpretation.

As just discussed, in calculating NOI, we do not deduct capital expenditures. Nor do we deduct mortgage payments. Therefore, NOI is the same for a property whether or not it has mortgage debt. Nonetheless, both capital expenditures and payments of mortgage principal and interest reduce the amount of actual net cash flow from the property because they are cash expenditures. They just are not considered operating expenses. Net cash flow is the actual remaining cash after deducting mortgage debt service and all capital items from NOI.

Net cash flow is the actual remaining cash after deducting mortgage debt service and all capital items from NOI.

You need to understand the importance of both NOI and net cash flow. NOI represents the operating results of your property and shows your effectiveness in generating income and controlling expenses. Net cash flow is your property-specific yardstick showing the amount of cash you are receiving from your property. Net cash flow is impacted by your interest rate, the terms of your mortgage, and the capital improvement expenditures you make.

As you will see in Chapter 5, there are four economic trends that directly influence property NOI. Three of these relate to rental demand and one to rental supply for any particular type of real estate at a given time in a given market. For example, if you own a rental home in a real estate market that has significant new job growth due to a new employer hiring people, you can probably raise the rent. This increase in demand drives the revenue portion of your NOI equation.

Expenses are generally less impacted by market trends, because they are largely a function of good management. Many of the expenses in real estate are relatively fixed and therefore cannot be dramatically cut. This is not to say that improving expense control, as we discuss in Chapter 11, is not an important opportunity for you as an investor.

The way NOI is valued during one time period can be totally different from another and is directly influenced by capitalization rate expectations. As the amount of money buyers are willing to pay for your stream of income (or NOI) changes, market cap rates adjust accordingly.

Using basic logic, most of us assume our real estate investment will demand a higher price if our property's NOI is higher than when we bought it. If you have made improvements, are charging higher rents, have lowered expenses, and have improved overall NOI, it is reasonable to assume you have created value. The fact is, however, that it's not quite that simple.

Capitalization Rates (Cap Rates)

Capitalization rate is the rate of return expected by an investor calculated by dividing annual property NOI by its sale price. (Remember that NOI does not include debt service or capital expenditures.)

Capitalization rate is the rate of return expected by an investor calculated by dividing annual property NOI by its sale price.

Cap rates give investors the ability to compare income streams from real estate with income streams from other investments, such as bond holdings. Cap rates do not represent total investor return, as most investors look for net annual returns in the range of 20% to 30%. I'll talk later in Chapter 8 about how these kinds of returns can be achieved (even when cap rates are in the 8%-10% range) through the use of leverage (mortgage debt on the property). Cap rates, like NOI, vary significantly by property type and by geographic region and can change materially over time, based on a multitude of factors.

CALCULATING CAP RATES

The cap rate for a property can be determined by dividing its annual NOI by its sale price. For example, if a property sells for $100,000 and has an annual NOI of $9,000, its cap rate would be 9%. Looking at it from another point of view, this also means that the property's NOI represents a 9% annual return on its sale price.

$$\frac{\$9,000 \text{ NOI}}{\$100,000 \text{ price}} = .09 \text{ or } 9\% \text{ cap rate}$$

How Cap Rates Impact Property Pricing

So if you agree with my principle that you don't make money owning real estate and you want to maximize the money you make when you sell, becoming more familiar with NOI and cap rates is key. NOI can be influenced through managing revenue and expenses, but cap rates have a greater effect on driving up (or down) the price of your real estate investments. This is why the prevailing cap rate at the time you sell your property is hugely important.

You can estimate the sales price on a property by using a cap rate that is typical for the property type and market area. Prevailing market cap rates can be found through a variety of sources, including local real estate brokers and other sources (e.g., the World Wide Web, published market studies, etc.). The formula presented earlier can be modified to calculate an estimated sale price. In this case, you would divide the NOI by the cap rate to calculate an estimated sales price for the property given the known approximate cap rate.

For example, if a property has a net operating income of $11,000 and the prevailing market cap rate is 8%, the estimated sale price for the property would be $137,500:

$$\frac{\$11,000 \text{ NOI}}{8\% \text{ (.08) cap rate}} = \$137,500 \text{ estimated sale price of property}$$

To demonstrate the dramatic difference in sale prices that results from different cap rates, see the next example, where the same property with the same NOI of $11,000 sold when the market had a prevailing cap rate of 9.5%:

$$\frac{\$11,000 \text{ NOI}}{9.5\% \text{ (.095) cap rate}} = \$115,789 \text{ estimated sale price for the property}$$

Cap rates are intended to be a rough yardstick and not an absolute, scientific way to compare returns among properties or with types of investments other than real estate. Since mortgage payments and capital expenditures are not factored into the cap rate calculations, actual cash flow is different, particularly depending on whether there's a mortgage or not. Having a mortgage, with its required mortgage payment, lowers net cash flow. However, as you are not investing the full cost of the property, under most circumstances having mortgage debt can actually increase your ultimate overall return—because you are investing far less up-front cash in the property.

Cap rates are intended to be a rough yardstick and not an absolute, scientific way to compare returns among properties or with types of investments other than real estate.

The pros and cons of mortgages and their impact on your investment return are addressed further in Chapter 8. But for now, suffice it to say that obtaining a long-term low-interest mortgage can be highly beneficial to your real estate investment. For example, if you have a property with an 8% fixed rate long-term mortgage that could be assumed by a buyer at a time when current mortgage interest rates are 11%, a buyer would likely accept a lower cap rate and pay extra for your property to obtain the favorable interest rate.

Having or not having mortgage debt will impact both your current cash returns and your overall investment return. As I argue throughout this book, your gain (or loss) on the sale of your property usually has a much greater impact than the cumulative cash flow on your overall return.

Why Lower Cap Rates Are Good

If you're selling property, when cap rates go down it's a good thing, in a somewhat counterintuitive way. The lower the cap rate, the higher the price. The higher the cap rate, the lower the price. Since cap rates represent a return on investment for a new purchaser, the lower the cap rate, the lower the income an investor is willing to accept in relation to the sale price. As a consequence, the lower the cap rate, the higher your sale price is in relation to the income being generated by your property.

Buy When Cap Rates Are High and Sell When They Are Low

To successfully time the market, one of your major goals as a real estate investor should be to buy when cap rates are high and sell when they are low. As with NOI, cap rates change over time. So, you may have increased your NOI significantly from the time you bought your property, but if cap rates also have gone up during that same time, you could end up selling at a loss. The following example shows how you can improve your property's NOI yet still not be able to sell it for more.

Let's assume that you bought the property discussed previously, which had an NOI of $11,000 for $137,500 when cap rates were 8%. Over the next three years, you did a great job with the property and increased the NOI to $15,000 per year. If cap rates were unchanged, you would have increased the likely sale price of your property to $187,500.

$$\frac{\$15,000 \text{ NOI}}{8\% \ (.08) \text{ cap rate}} = \$187,500 \text{ prospective sales price}$$

However, if market conditions changed and the prevailing cap rates for your property type in this market went from 8% to 11%, meaning that prospective buyers would be demanding a higher cash return on the property in relation to its purchase price, this would equate to a sale price of $136,364.

$$\frac{\$9,000 \text{ NOI}}{11\% \ (.11) \text{ cap rate}} = \$136,364 \text{ prospective sale price}$$

Using this scenario, even though you increased the net income of the property by a very impressive 36% (from $11,000 to $15,000), the price of the property (if you sold it then) actually had declined slightly from your original purchase price. This illustrates the need to understand real estate cycles and to time your sales and purchases accordingly.

When most people buy income-producing real estate, they focus exclusively on increasing the NOI of the property. While this is an important task in terms of improving value, fluctuating cap rates can have a much greater impact on your prospective sale price for the property than its NOI. Buying and selling at the right time is critical. The next chapter will help you recognize "the right time."

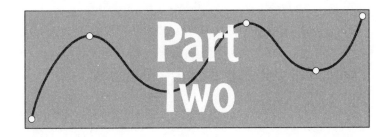

Part Two

The Seven Trends That Drive Real Estate Timing Decisions

The Seven Major Trends Behind Real Estate Cycles

Real estate pricing cycles are continuously influenced by a combination of seven major forces or trends. The dominance of one trend over another and the interaction of the trends cause cycle movement and change. Real estate cycles vary in duration and severity, with high points and low points differing greatly from cycle to cycle. Each cycle is different, yet understanding the effects of the trends can help you understand where you are in a cycle and how best to proceed.

Understanding the effects of the trends can help you understand where you are in a cycle and how best to proceed.

The seven trends fall into two primary categories: national and local. The first three trends—inflation, interest rates, and "flow of funds"—operate primarily on a national level. The last four—job growth, migration, "path of progress," and new construction—operate primarily on a local level. National trends more directly impact capitalization rates and only indirectly impact NOI. Local trends affect both NOI and cap rates. Regardless, it is the collective interaction that moves prices and causes variances in highs and lows and in cycle duration.

In the discussion and charts that follow, I give you my views on how the seven trends impact property pricing. This includes how each trend in isolation impacts NOI and cap rates. I also provide hypothetical examples of the directions and impact of each trend.

The Three National Trends

Three national trends—inflation, interest rates, and capital flow—affect real estate cycles in a broad, general way and can impact directly whether any given real estate investment is more successful or more likely to end up costing you money. Buying real estate against the trends can produce favorable results, but this decision must be made with great care and understanding of what influences the trends. Buying with these trends on your side can turn what might have been an average investment into a superior one.

Each of the three national trends is unique. If you study them together over time, you will be able to recognize powerful benchmarks that can help you make thoughtful investment decisions.

None of these trends directly affects the way your property NOIs are calculated, but each in its own way indirectly affects the amount of NOI generated. More directly, they impact how properties are priced. But their primary influence is on market cap rate expectations. Higher interest rates and higher cap rates that often accompany times of inflationary growth lead investors to expect greater rates of return. While this rule of thumb is important to understand, generalizations like this can be dangerous, as you will soon discover. Forecasting trends is an art, not a science, but it can and must be done.

National Trend #1: Inflation

During the late 1960s and early 1970s, inflation was known as "the friend of real estate." Though this idea remains theoretically simple, sound, and fundamentally true, it's not always the case.

During the day-to-day course of the real estate business, if prices of lumber and other raw materials used in the construction process rise, construction and replacement costs on improved real estate go up accordingly. Similarly, with inflation we are able to increase the amount we charge in rent. What we would like, obviously, is for rents to rise faster than expenses. This is commonly referred to as "NOI increasing at or above inflationary rates."

If inflation goes up slowly over a period of time, property values should generally stay in step. If NOI on a property at the time of purchase were $100,000 per year and increased an average of 3% per year without compounding, at the end of five years NOI would have gone up to $115,000. The extra $15,000 could be looked at as an "inflationary increase in NOI." If rents were increasing faster than inflation, the increase in NOI could be the result of rents going up $30,000 while expenses went up $15,000, with a positive result of $15,000.

One important point to remember is that inflation does not affect everything equally. Room rates at hotels, for example, can be adjusted upward daily, whereas a one-year apartment lease sets the monthly rental amount for that period of time. Similarly, expenses go up and at times even down based only indirectly on inflation. Generally, U.S. real estate income and expenses are not indexed or tied directly to inflation, but instead are driven by market supply-and-demand factors. These factors are influenced by inflation, but inconsistently. As a property owner, your goal is to have inflation increase your rents to a greater percentage than your expenses. The result you want is to have your NOI increases actually exceed the rate of inflation on a percentage basis.

Inflation also directly affects real estate replacement costs, which in turn ultimately affect property prices. If the costs associated with new construction (materials, labor, legal, and permit costs) are rising, prices of existing property are positively impacted. During times of deflation, this works in reverse. If you could build a brand-new house for less than an existing house on a lot right next door, why would you buy the existing house? The answer is, you wouldn't. So sellers of existing property have to reduce their prices to a level lower than the new house. As long as the inflation trend is going upward along with replacement costs and NOI, inflation is the friend of real estate.

INFLATION CAN TRANSFER RISK FROM REAL ESTATE INVESTORS TO LENDERS

Inflation and interest rates usually work hand in hand. As inflation goes, interest rates likely will follow.

However, often there is a gap in timing before interest rates rise that can be problematic for lenders. Lenders expect a certain return on their money over a period of years; that expectation is influenced by current and perceived future inflation. If an investor buys a property with a fixed interest rate and then a period of inflation follows, the investor benefits and the lender loses ground.

For example, if you purchase a property for $1 million with a fixed 7% loan for $800,000 and then inflation moves NOI from its initial $100,000 at a rate of 4% per year to $120,000, you as the owner will benefit. But for the lender, with a fixed rate of 7% and an inflationary increase of 4%, the "real rate of return" generated on its loan turns out to be a net of only 3%. While you as the owner have an unlimited upside in this scenario, the lender's benefit is limited.

Capturing inflationary benefits is one of the great objectives in real estate transactions. You can't always realize these benefits, because we have no crystal balls and timing may work against you. Mortgage lenders can require floating interest rates that go up and down based on changes in the market, set penalties for future changes in interest rates, or simply demand extremely high rates for fixed mortgages. All these actions can deprive borrowers of inflationary benefits. In theory, each of these factors comes into play when rates and terms of mortgage interest are negotiated.

Capturing inflationary benefits is one of the great objectives in real estate transactions.

Generally speaking, during markets with rising inflation, if you have a mortgage with a fixed interest rate, you'll come out ahead. Borrowing for a period of 10 years or longer at fixed rates in a period of moderately increasing inflation is a recipe for a good real estate investment.

Too Much Inflation Can Hurt You

While inflation is a true friend to real estate investing most of the time, there are exceptions. Rapid rates of inflation can wreak havoc on real estate, as in the mid 1970s, when inflation grew at a rate of over 10% per year. For one thing, expenses will tend to grow more quickly than you can raise rents. As mentioned previously, an exception is the hospitality industry, where rates can be changed daily. Rents on most other property types can be raised only at the end of lease periods. In the apartment sector, this could be as early as six months to a year, but in the office sector, leases are often signed for five- and 10-year periods. Utilities, insurance, maintenance, and other property service costs fluctuate more frequently. Consequently, without the ability to adjust rents accordingly, you could experience a rapid decline in property NOI.

For example, if you started out with a healthy $100,000 NOI and expenses rose faster than you were able to increase rents, over a five-year period the NOI on the same property could drop to $85,000. So, as you can see, high levels of rapidly increasing inflation on some types of real estate can backfire, putting extreme pressure on NOI.

There are other more significant issues that accompany high levels of inflation and perceived future inflation. Lenders, wanting to protect their investments while making deals, will agree to fixed-rate mortgages during times of moderate inflation. But when inflation is high and/or rising, lenders often prefer shorter-term loans or loans with floating rates. Mortgages that adjust the rate every three or four years or that float every 90 days to six months can transfer the benefits of inflation from the owner/borrower to the lender. Lenders view adjustable rate mortgages as reasonable protection. If a borrower believes inflation is a friend, during times of too much inflation, this perspective can backfire.

THE PERFECT INFLATIONARY TREND

As Figure 5-1 indicates, situations in which lenders perceive stability and moderate rates of inflation are probably the friendliest to the real estate investor. When inflation is trending to very high or very low levels, the challenge goes to the owner. The tricky time for the real estate investor is deflation. It is clearly not the friend of real estate.

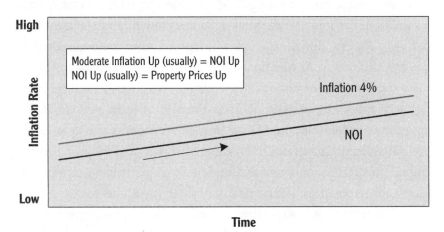

Figure 5-1. Moderate inflation, impact on NOI

Cap rates generally benefit—i.e., go down—at moderate inflation levels, as demonstrated in Figure 5-2. But once inflation becomes extreme, either as hyperinflation or as deflation, cap rates turn negative—i.e., go up. If prices of newly constructed real estate go down

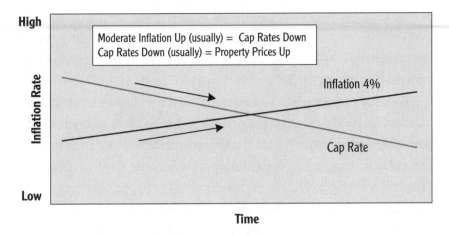

Figure 5-2. Moderate inflation, impact on cap rates

in value (as they did in some areas in 2003), cap rates start going up and existing, highly leveraged real estate can become a financial risk.

As this book is being written, we are experiencing a period of inflation/deflation stress. Certain economic sectors are inflating while others are deflating, due in large part to changes brought about by new technologies and the impact of the stock market bubble of 2000. Investing requires considering, among other things, the future of inflation or deflation. My personal prediction, though subject to changing information and certainly not something I would encourage you to bet heavily on, is that this current deflationary period will soon end and inflation will be on its way back.

National Trend #2: Interest Rates

Most real estate is purchased with a mortgage. That you can borrow heavily on real estate is generally considered one of its biggest investment benefits. If you can finance 70% or more of a property's purchase price, you gain a distinct advantage over many other investment alternatives. This is particularly true if your interest rate on the amount financed is less than prevailing market cap rates. For example, if your $1 million property were earning 9% at the time of purchase (i.e., had a cap rate of nine), your return would be $90,000. If your mortgage were financed at a fixed interest rate of 7%, you would be keeping the 2% per year increase in value on the amount you financed.

There are times when money is borrowed at higher interest rates than cap rates. This is frequently the case during times of higher inflation. The theory is that NOI will increase over time, so it's worthwhile to receive a lower return for a short period because improvements are expected over the long haul. It doesn't always happen that way, but at least there is hope at the beginning of the investment period.

Interest rates are an extraordinarily powerful and important part of the structure of any real estate investment. In general, as Figure 5-3 and Figure 5-4 show, lower rates are better for real estate investments because they result in lower cap rates and provide other desired economic benefits. For example, a direct economic benefit comes from the fact that low interest rates reduce mortgage debt payments and allow borrowers to take on more debt (bigger property loans) than when interest rates are higher. As discussed earlier, low and moderate inflation rates generally keep interest rates low, as borrowers do not demand high rates for fear of inflation.

Interest rates are an extraordinarily powerful and important part of the structure of any real estate investment.

Long-term fixed rates during moderately rising inflationary periods can provide great opportunities for success. During this time period, inflation's positive benefits can occur while interest rates remain stable. (See left side of Figure 5-3.)

The situation changes when the perception of lenders is that they need to raise rates faster to protect themselves against inflation. In this circumstance, cap rates also increase, albeit on a lagging basis, in a manner that is negative to real estate pricing. (See right side of Figure 5-3.)

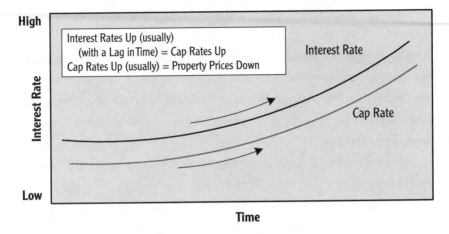

Figure 5-3. Impact of increasing interest rates

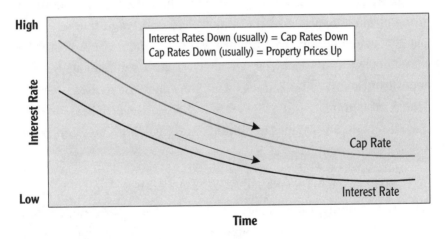

Figure 5-4. Impact of decreasing interest rates

When interest rates are higher, cap rates trend higher as well, driving down property prices.

THE "GOTCHA CLAUSES"

Lenders over the past couple of decades have realized that simple mortgages with fixed interest rates and no loan prepayment penalties give all of the benefits of declining interest rates to the borrower. Many investors who buy properties during times when interest rates are high attempt to refinance their mortgages as interest rates go down.

Today, many commercial loans are written so that the borrower can't prepay the loan during an initial time period. Most lenders, in fact, charge significant penalties for early refinancing or early payoff. One such common penalty is referred to as "yield maintenance." At the time of refinancing, a yield maintenance penalty requires the borrower to pay the lender the difference between what the lender would have made if the loan had stayed in place and what the lender could make today if the money were reinvested in a treasury note for the same duration. These penalties can be very expensive.

Penalties for early refinancing are less common on loans on single-family houses. If you buy a single-family home for use as a rental property and finance it in the mainstream mortgage market, you'll usually have the option to refinance without penalty. A 1% closing fee is customary, and other costs associated with refinancing (escrow deposits, title insurance, surveys, etc.) may decrease modestly the net benefit of refinancing a single-family home. Nevertheless, overall, there are great advantages to holding mortgages with no interest rate prepayment penalties.

Low Interest Rates Aren't Always a Plus

While low interest rates are generally good for real estate, in some circumstances they're bad for apartment properties. In many market areas, when interest rates are at a low level in a cycle, apartments suffer because many of their more economically stable residents are able to move into the single-family market.

As you can see from Figure 5-5, significant declines in interest rates are detrimental to apartment owners. In the late 1990s and early 2000s, a combination of declining and extraordinarily low interest rates together with very modest down payment requirements motivated many apartment residents to buy homes. It was simply less expensive to own a home than to lease a premium apartment.

In fact, not long ago I met with an old friend who had developed a wonderful luxury apartment community in 1998. It opened fully occupied with high rental rates. Just four years later, after interest rates had fallen, residents had moved out in droves to buy homes. The only thing he could do to keep people in the complex was to significantly reduce rents. At the same time, his 8% loan included one of those "gotcha clauses." He simply could not prepay the loan. While current rates were less than 6%, he was stuck at 8%. Not only was he losing money, he also was faced with a possible default on the mortgage.

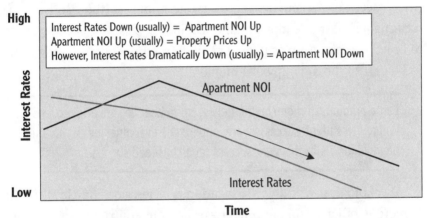

Interest Rates Down (usually) = Apartment NOI Up
Apartment NOI Up (usually) = Property Prices Up
However, Interest Rates Dramatically Down (usually) = Apartment NOI Down

Reason: dramatically lower interest rates increase numbers of people buying single-family homes as an alternative to renting, creating higher apartment vacancies.

Figure 5-5. Impact of lower interest rates on apartments

National Trend #3: Flow of Funds

Flow of funds can seem like a fickle phenomenon. Sometimes (especially after a stock market crash) investing in real estate is more popular than investing elsewhere, which drives up prices. Also, during a given period, investors will favor one property type over others, driving up the pricing of properties of that type. Investors also have a herd mentality and move with a common sense of direction. This doesn't mean they all get together and decide to invest in real estate instead of the stock market or decide to buy shopping centers instead of land, but masses of investment capital can and does flow in the same direction.

If we look at the world as containing a huge but finite amount of money, it's important to understand how that capital is allocated. Where is the money, what is it invested in, and where is it going? Capital obviously flows into different sectors (tech stocks, foreign stocks, bonds, etc.) at different times, with investors not always in agreement on a common course of action. Still, large amounts of money ultimately seem to head in similar directions. When investment successes are publicized, everyone jumps on the bandwagon, creating a shift in the movement of capital. In this way, success tends to breed success. And, as people begin to see prices go up, they want to be part of the new upward momentum.

Large amounts of money ultimately seem to head in similar directions. When investment successes are publicized, everyone jumps on the bandwagon .... In this way, success tends to breed success.

Psychological worldviews, taxation policies, currency levels, and numerous other factors at any given moment contribute to the flow of funds into real estate. As Figure 5-6 represents, when more money goes into real estate and available property remains constant, cap rates go down and prices go up. The reverse is also true. As money turns away from real estate, cap rates go up and prices go down.

WHEN STOCKS ARE HOT, REAL ESTATE IS NOT

While it's not an absolute, it's fair to say that when the stock market is booming, real estate is not. Throughout the 1990s, as the stock market continued on its seemingly endless rise, investor interest in real estate declined. With only so much money to allocate, if investors perceive greater opportunity in the stock market, they'll reduce their percentage of funds flowing into other areas, including real estate.

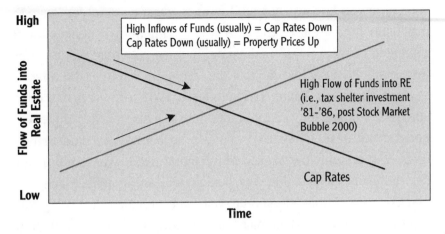

Figure 5-6. Effect of flow of funds into real estate

The opposite is also true. When the market began to crash in 2000, we started seeing an increase in investor interest in real estate. In addition to reacting to their losses in the market, some investors perceived real estate to be a more tangible and reliable investment. But is running from one to the other wise?

For many, I believe, it only makes matters worse. Jumping into real estate at a time when values are already at moderate to high levels only results in overpaying for assets. Many people investing in real estate, if they are not cautious, will get burned just as they did in the stock market. Furthermore, real estate is more difficult to sell than stocks—and almost impossible to get out of on short notice. Redirecting large amounts of money from stocks into real estate can set you up for disaster. There are clearly opportunities, but caution and a thorough consideration of timing and trends are critical both to protect your investment and to set yourself up for higher-than-average returns.

THE IMPACT OF TAX INCENTIVES

The Economic Recovery Tax Act of 1981 encouraged investment in real estate. Depreciation was shortened and accelerated, and the resulting paper losses were extraordinarily beneficial to investors.

Soon after this law was passed, I wrote a guest editorial for *Barron's* that likened creation of the new law to ringing a bell signaling a stampede of money into real estate. It came at a time when prices were generally very low, making the idea seem sound at the time.

Many investors heard that bell. From 1981 through 1986, huge amounts of money flowed into real estate as a direct result of the Act. But the tax benefits realized couldn't be considered fundamental parts of the cash flow supply-and-demand cycle, which ultimately determines property value. Tax benefits are an intangible incentive that Congress simply added on to normal economics, disrupting true supply and demand dynamics. But, as long as they existed, they would benefit investors.

But what if the government changed its mind? That's exactly what happened. The Tax Reform Act of 1986 abruptly and retroactively changed the rules of the game. Investors who were counting on using real estate losses to offset ordinary income could no longer take the losses. Accordingly, the huge flow of funds into real estate dried up immediately.

Essentially, the game changed while in progress, and these drastic changes in flow of funds killed the real estate market. Anyone who didn't or couldn't sell their assets quickly in 1986 watched real estate prices plummet in 1987, 1988, and beyond. The flow of funds had stopped flowing. Prices went down as cap rates went up. While the flow of funds was not solely responsible for this real estate crash, it was a huge contributing factor.

THE ROLE OF FOREIGN MONEY AND MONEY MANAGERS

While the vast majority of money flowing into U.S. real estate is from U.S. investors, funds also come from foreign sources. Depending on where our dollar stands relative to other currencies and the economic conditions of their countries, foreign investors with excess capital historically have contributed to the money flowing into U.S. real estate.

The Seven Major Trends Behind Real Estate Cycles

During the mid 1970s, Middle Eastern oil money entered the U.S. real estate markets. The good news for us was that this capital infusion cushioned an otherwise serious down period.

In the mid 1980s when real estate prices were just starting to decline, the last buyers to pay high prices turned out to be the Japanese. With excess capital from a strong yen and a robust economy, these investors were out in force, overpaying for U.S. real estate at the very top of the market. They were motivated by their ability to borrow money in Japan at very low interest rates, buy real estate here, and enjoy positive cash flow in spite of extremely high purchase prices. Paying much more than any U.S. investor would pay, Japanese investors bought a number of golf courses and high-profile buildings across the country. You may remember, for instance, that Japanese investors bought Rockefeller Center in New York. This flow of money from Japan into our real estate markets helped bail out many troubled properties. Unfortunately for the Japanese investors, only a short time later their stock market collapsed, causing a serious economic downturn. They needed their investment capital and were forced to sell their U.S. assets in a down cycle. Many experienced huge losses; others lost everything through foreclosure.

Similar to the impact of foreign funds on the U.S. real estate market, changes in money flow can result from strategic decisions made by committees of people responsible for investing other people's money. Pension fund managers, for example, reviewing stock market and other losses from the early 2000s, made decisions to increase allocations to real estate. To show the magnitude of the impact this can have on the real estate market, assume CalPERS (California Public Employees' Retirement System)—a pension fund with total investments of $150 billion—increased its real estate allocation by just 1%, the result would be an additional flow of funds of $1.5 billion. Collectively, if many pension funds increase their allocations from stock to real estate by just a few percentage points, it would dramatically impact the real estate market.

It's important to note that, as intermediaries, most money managers make money only if transactions occur. Therefore, they may have incentives to buy and sell assets beyond pure investment economics. As an investor, beware of the buying competition in an aggressive environment involving intermediaries managing money for others. Similarly, be cautious when competing with other special interest groups willing to pay high prices based on their own unique motivations.

Beware of the buying competition in an aggressive environment involving intermediaries managing money for others. Similarly, be cautious when competing with other special interest groups willing to pay high prices based on their own unique motivations.

In any given marketplace, there's usually a buyer with a higher and better use for the investment than you—and they might not always be right. The Japanese investors turned out to be wrong, as did the buyers in the early 1980s who were depending on the government's promises. Today we may see a similar trend from investors disenchanted with the stock market. Will they be right or wrong? Only time will tell, but hopefully this book will help shed some light on both the opportunities and the risks.

PSYCHOLOGY PLAYS A BIG ROLE

What's going on inside each investor's mind also influences the market. In 2000, at the turn of the year, the NASDAQ exceeded 5,000. In April, the dramatic crash began and the NASDAQ fell over the next three years more than 75% from its high in 2000. The stock market's decade-long expansion and extraordinary highs had made it the first choice for individual and institutional investors alike in the 1990s. But, comparable only to the 1930s, great wealth was quickly destroyed as the market fell. At that point, the stunned and leery investment community experienced a definite shift in mindset.

Interestingly, real estate investment trusts (REITs) have been one of the better-performing sectors within the stock market over the past few years. Many investors have turned to this investment vehicle to gain exposure to real estate in their investment portfolio. Yet most people interested in real estate favor more direct investment methods. Partly because of low interest rates, investments in single-family homes have been booming, causing some to worry that the boom is just a bubble waiting to burst. From my perspective, single-family homes are not likely to suffer a major decline in value on a widespread basis, though local market cycles differ considerably. We also see renewed interest in second homes as investments, as many investors recognize the dual benefit of having a second home for enjoyment as well as a place to park capital as an alternative to the stock market.

Investor psychology does not open the money spout instantaneously, but instead turns it on slowly over time. Just as when an individual decides to invest in a second home, a limited partnership, or directly in smaller rental properties, that same psychology is at work when individuals make decisions on behalf of pension funds and institutional investors. These third-party decisions can have a more profound effect on the market than your decision whether to buy a second home. As we look forward to the balance of the first decade of the 21st century, it's likely that investor psychology will continue on its current course, generating greater influx of money into real estate.

THE IMPACT OF LOWER INTEREST RATES ON FLOW OF FUNDS

In addition to the obvious impact of interest rates, there are also other, more esoteric influences on real estate investment. When large companies with direct or indirect real estate investments find that their rates of return are hurt due to declining interest rates, they look for alternative ways to participate in the industry. Their desire for higher returns can lead to innovative and interesting—though perhaps ultimately dangerous—approaches to real estate investing.

Since early 2000, these innovative approaches continue to increase the flow of money into real estate.

Some companies are creating agreements with developers to acquire existing real estate. In some of these joint venture arrangements, the institutional company puts up 95% of the money and the developer puts up 5%. The company expects to get its money back plus a 6% or 7% return, with the partners sharing profits 50/50 thereafter.

For example, a partnership might be structured with the institutional partner putting $95 million and the real estate developer contributing $5 million. The venture is then able to borrow 75% or more to finance purchases. In this way, the joint venture could acquire a total of $400 million in real estate ($100 million in equity plus $300 million in borrowed funds), and the developer would have only $5 million at risk, which could be recouped quickly from management and other fees.

This approach can turn out well for both developer and institutional investor, with the investor ultimately becoming an equity owner and partner in properties it could not have developed and purchases on its own. In some scenarios, investors may take a value approach and look for Class B properties, usually older or with operating problems, in weakened markets to rehabilitate and sell when times improve. While many of these transactions will allow the involved parties to make money, others will fail. Either way, the theory behind this approach is based on the current low interest-rate environment.

Lenders in a very low interest-rate environment will look to creative new strategies like this one to get a higher overall return. When interest rates are higher, my experience has been that most lenders are satisfied with their returns without looking to complicated and riskier joint venture financing structures.

The Four Local Trends

Generalities can be dangerous and for every rule there are exceptions. But one of the things that makes real estate enjoyable to me is that each property is unique. No matter how similar one property may seem to another, ultimately, property type and particular location define the viability of each real estate investment. The four local trends—job growth, migration, path of progress, and new construction—play significant roles in the uniqueness of your investment and the likelihood of obtaining a large return on it.

One of the things that makes real estate enjoyable to me is that each property is unique.

Still, what's good for apartments may be bad for retail or vice versa. Within any given area, you'll typically find vast differences in what is good or bad for different property types. Hotels, office buildings, apartments, single-family homes, and retail are all different real estate product types, each with its own unique functions. If the apartment market is overbuilt in one area, it may be good if you own a retail store nearby but not so good if you own apartments.

Also within any given market area, various types of real estate may be affected differently during the same period of time. For instance, in Dallas, in 2002, home prices rose by 4.2% while prices for office buildings were falling, reflecting an increase in vacancies. This huge disparity in price movement exemplifies the diverse character of real estate investments.

Each type of real estate must be considered carefully within its specific local market area. Clearly, once you have evaluated the status of the three national trends, it's time to take a closer look at the local markets. Within every city, as we all know, there are better and worse locations for owning property and the preferred locations change over time. What we think is a hot location today could be seen as inferior in a matter of 10 or 15 years.

One of our early successful markets in the multi-family sector was Albuquerque. Our properties were right in the heart of the action. Within 10 years, a whole new area of the city had been developed, putting our investments and us on the wrong side of the tracks. We learned just how much local trends matter.

What follows is a discussion of the four trends that impact real estate more on a local level.

Local Trend #1: Job Growth

One of the strongest trends impacting the demand for real estate is job growth. This trend directly correlates with apartment occupancy levels, retail sales per square foot, single-family home sales and rentals, and office occupancies. Job growth drives real estate demand and, in turn, increases NOIs. As shown in Figure 5-7, positive job growth, assuming all other trends remain constant, has a powerful influence on increasing NOI and ultimately on property pricing. As Figure 5-8 shows, the reverse is also true.

You can learn about job growth in your local market through city and county government offices, including economic development departments. Look at comparative job growth statistics over at least

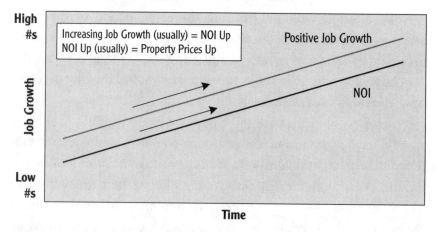

Figure 5-7. Impact of positive job growth

The Seven Major Trends Behind Real Estate Cycles

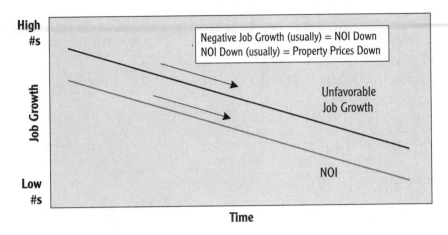

Figure 5-8. Impact of negative job growth

a period of five years. A review of the ups and downs in job growth will have much to do with the success or failure of many types of real estate in that area.

Local Trend #2: In- or Out-Migration

Similar to job growth, in-migration creates demand for the use of many types of real estate. It will, for instance, impact apartment rentals, home sales, retail sales, and so on. In addition to local market in-migration, demographics play a role in understanding this trend. Are those moving in (or out) young or old? What are their income levels? What about their levels of education? What are their buying needs and desires?

In-migration creates real estate demand that can help forecast specific real estate successes. If an area has just experienced in-migration of people with relatively low incomes, the demand for rental housing is likely to be higher than the demand for new single-family residences. If the in-migration consists of people in their 50s or nearing retirement age, they are more likely to be home owners or even residents of senior living facilities. Whether the people are relocating for jobs, retirement, or other reasons, it's important to know something about them.

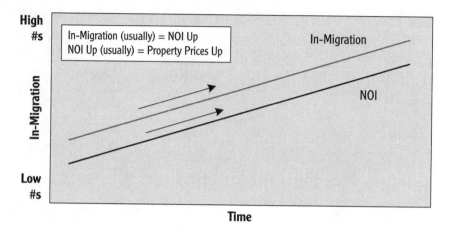

Figure 5-9. Impact of in-migration

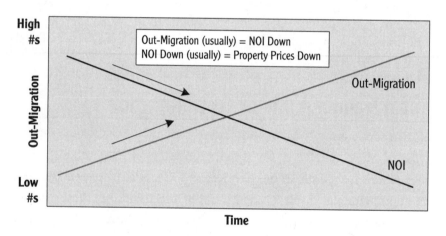

Figure 5-10. Impact of out-migration

As Figure 5-9 and Figure 5-10 show, positive in-migration increases rental demand and, in turn, NOI and, ultimately, property prices. Out-migration decreases rental demand and, in turn, NOI and property prices as well.

Local Trend #3: Path of Progress

Within cities there are areas that fall in a "path of progress," and there are other areas that are stagnant. For example, in the Dallas area, growth has for quite some time been heading straight north. We made several strategic land purchases in 1989 based on this specific trend.

One was the purchase of 175 acres of undeveloped land on the far northwest fringe of the metropolitan area. We held this land for roughly 10 years, until all other multifamily parcels in the area had been developed. We bought when demand was low and sold when demand—and the value of the land—had risen substantially.

Also back around 1989, we purchased a 162-acre parcel of land in the small town of Frisco, at the north end of Dallas's major north/south artery, the Dallas North Tollway. Some joked that we had just bought land in Oklahoma. But in 1997, betting further on the path of progress trend, we designed a four-million-square-foot master plan for a unique office community to be built over a 15-year period. When Hall Office Park opened in late 1998 with the first 100,000-square-foot office building, I was still getting inquiries about the state of my sanity. Early in the construction phase, roads were so impassable we had to take our prospects to see the building in four-wheel-drive vehicles. But by 1998, the Tollway was being expanded and we had completely leased that first building in six months. It wasn't long before it was obvious to everyone that Hall Office Park was in the heart of the new real estate action.

In contrast, in late 1999, Dallas as a whole had a huge surplus of office space, with more under construction. This continued throughout 2000. By 2002, the Dallas metropolitan area had an office building vacancy rate of approximately 25%. Building owners everywhere suffered. By this time, we had completed eight buildings totaling more than one million square feet at Hall Office Park. At a time when most landlords were losing tenants due to an economic recession and the decline of the high tech industry, Hall Office Park was signing leases to creditworthy tenants such as General Electric, EADS TELECOM North America, and Fujitsu Transaction Solutions. We were in the path of progress and, even

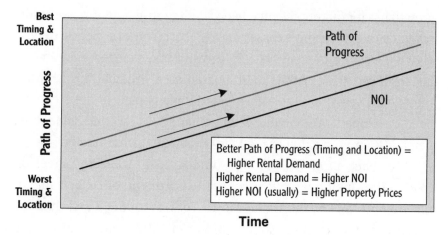

Figure 5-11. Impact of being in the path of progress

though the market area as a whole was not doing well, we were uniquely positioned to benefit.

As Figure 5-11 illustrates, being in the path of progress increases rental demand, NOI, and, ultimately, property prices.

Local Trend #4: New Construction

Job growth, in-migration, and path of progress trends are indicators that create real estate demand. New construction deals with the opposite influence—supply. New construction can be a reasonably predictable trend. For example, too much or too little supply of specific real estate types in any given market can cause NOIs to go up or down as rental demand strengthens or weakens. As Figure 5-12 shows, new construction that exceeds demand can have a devastating impact on NOI.

From 1998 to 2002, with new office space still being built in Dallas and vacancies increasing, it was easy to predict that our general oversupply of office space would continue to get worse. What was not predictable was the impact of national economic events or even the events themselves. Recession impacts real estate demand—and a national recession combined with local market oversupply can be deadly for investors.

The Seven Major Trends Behind Real Estate Cycles

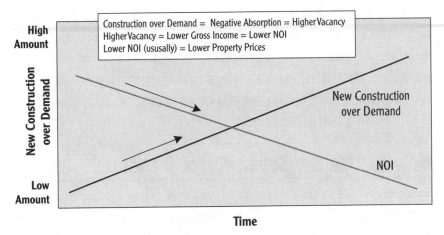

Figure 5-12. Impact of excessive new construction over demand

Unlike my company, most real estate developers are intermediaries. They're not generally building with their own money for their own account. Instead, they're usually building on borrowed money and with the hope that one day soon they'll make some money by selling the property. From this perspective, developers often give very little thought to the actual current or future demand for the property. Instead, they focus on their ability to get a project going and completed and on the fees and/or profits they hope to make along the way.

Overbuilding—just at the wrong time—characterizes cycle after cycle. But the 100-year flood of the 1980s left so many deep scars that the lending community was forced to make some serious changes.

Unfortunately, lenders hold the reins when it comes to slowing new construction, and, historically, they haven't held on too tightly. Overbuilding—just at the wrong time—characterizes cycle after cycle. But the 100-year flood of the 1980s left so many deep scars that the lending community was forced to make some serious changes. In the 1990s and 2000s, we've seen lenders pay more attention to trends, demographics, and demand for real estate before financing new projects.

Watching the actions of lenders can signal investment opportunity. As I write this book, some lenders are shying away from the hospitality market sector based primarily on a global downturn in performance. By pulling back early enough, these lenders actually will contribute to a more orderly cycle of demand than we might have seen if they'd continued to lend freely.

How to Use the Seven Major Trends

Each of the seven major trends affects real estate cycles. But to see how these trends can affect individual investors, we must examine three issues more closely. In Chapter 6 we will look at the practical decisions that result from the direction of each trend and how the seven trends interact. In Chapter 7 we'll cover how you decide where your particular property purchase or sale fits into a cycle. In later chapters, I'll discuss how to use the knowledge of these trends and real estate cycles with different philosophical approaches toward buying, holding, or selling real estate.

What Each of the Seven Trends Tells You About When to Buy, Hold, or Sell

I used to joke with my children about how simple real estate investing was: the goal was merely to buy low, sell high, and keep the difference. While indeed it sounds simple, in practice, it sure can be difficult. The secret is in the timing.

In this chapter, when I talk about buy, hold, or sell positions for each of the seven trends, I am presupposing that all other trends and all other aspects of a decision would be neutral, that the only thing impacting the decision at that point is the particular trend in question. This supposition helps us understand what the impact of each trend should be on our practical decisions. In reality, of course, all other things are never neutral. It's necessary to understand each trend in a pure form, but in a real transaction it's also necessary to consider the interaction of all of the trends. Throughout the balance of the book, I'll address the interaction of the trends and how they ultimately lead to real estate cycles.

For the purposes of discussing trends within this chapter, I have excluded what might be considered personal motivations and circumstances. For example, even if it is not the ideal time to sell according to the trends, if you need cash, you may just have to sell anyway. There are situations that take precedence over where your property stands in the cycles, but even so, you are better off understanding the effects of timing.

It's necessary to understand each trend in a pure form, but in a real transaction it's also necessary to consider the interaction of all of the trends.

The sections that follow summarize my investing recommendations for each type of property (houses, apartments, land, office buildings, retail, and hotels and motels) based on each of the seven trends.

Timing Recommendations for Single-Family, Rental, and Second Homes

Single-family homes are unique in that they often have lower cap rates than other types of real estate. This is probably because the highest and best use for most single-family homes is perceived to be use by the owner, as opposed to renters who would generate income.

Single-family homes may seem like a safe investment, but that is not always the case. Like many other lessons, I learned this one the hard way.

Many years ago, during a down time in the Flint, Michigan housing market, my brother-in-law, who lived there, approached me with the idea of buying single-family homes at depressed prices for investment purposes. We proceeded to buy 40 homes over a couple of years. The investments were disasters. Rental income during our period of ownership continued to fall because job losses in the auto industry were causing migration out of Flint to other areas. From this venture, I learned two very difficult but important lessons the hard way: not every down market turns around and you should sell—not buy—when there is out-migration.

Trend #1. Inflation

Moderate (1% to 10%)

Recommendation for Single-Family Homes: Buy, Sell, or Hold

Qualifications/Reasoning/Comments: This level of inflation has a neutral influence on single-family houses. Decisions should depend upon personal circumstances and other market conditions.

Hyperinflation (>10%)

Recommendation for Single-Family Homes: Hold or Sell

Qualifications/Reasoning/Comments: Buying in this environment is risky, because prices already have risen dramatically and lenders are likely to require more onerous terms to protect themselves from the impact of inflation. Your downside if you buy near the top of the inflation trend is painful.

Deflation (<0%)

Recommendation for Single-Family Homes: Sell

Qualifications/Reasoning/Comments: Deflation causes prices to decline, so you would want to sell at the earliest indication. While mortgage costs stay the same, property prices will fall.

Trend #2. Interest Rates

Low to Moderate (5% to 10%)

Recommendation for Single-Family Homes: Buy, Sell, or Hold

Qualifications/Reasoning/Comments: This level of interest rate is favorable for buying, selling, or holding. However, extremely low interest rates would tend toward selling. Interest rates do not stay at the lowest end for extended periods. When interest rates begin to go higher, housing prices are usually negatively impacted, though often with a lag in timing.

High (>10%)

Recommendation for Single-Family Homes: Hold or Sell

Qualifications/Reasoning/Comments: When interest rates are high, it's generally not a good time to buy, because mortgage payments will be much higher than at lower rates. Selling is a good option, particularly if you have an assumable loan with a lower interest rate, giving the purchaser a reason to pay a premium for the property. (Many single-family loans are assumable, but you should read each mortgage carefully. The terms will specify whether or not the loan is assumable.)

TREND #3. FLOW OF FUNDS

Flow In

Recommendation for Single-Family Homes: Buy or Hold

Qualifications/Reasoning/Comments: When money is flowing into real estate, you want to be buying or holding. If the flow is in the early stage, you want to buy. If the trend is well established, you may want to hold until you sense a shift in the tide; then it's time to sell.

Flow Out

Recommendation for Single-Family Homes: Sell or Hold

Qualifications/Reasoning/Comments: When money is beginning to flow out of real estate, you want to sell. If you're late in the cycle, prices probably have already declined and you should hold.

TREND #4. JOB GROWTH

Steady or Increasing

Recommendation for Single-Family Homes: Buy or Hold

Qualifications/Reasoning/Comments: Steady or increasing job growth is one of the most positive trends for single-family homes. New jobs bring in people who need places to live. If job growth appears likely to continue for the near term, you should hold homes or buy homes.

Negative or Rapid Decline

Recommendation for Single-Family Homes: Sell

Qualifications/Reasoning/Comments: If job growth slows or there is a loss of jobs in a market, it's a strong signal to sell. A rapid decline in the rate of positive job growth is often a signal that job losses are next.

TREND #5. MIGRATION

Into the Area

Recommendation for Single-Family Homes: Buy or Hold

Qualifications/Reasoning/Comments: In-migration is universally good for the single-family home market. Buy if the trend appears likely to continue for some time, but keep in mind that demographics play a supporting role. If most of the newcomers are low-income families, apartments likely will benefit more than single-family homes, with the possible exception of starter homes.

Out of the Area

Recommendation for Single-Family Homes: Sell

Qualifications/Reasoning/Comments: When people start leaving the area, sell immediately. Net out-migration is never good for the single-family market. Once out-migration begins, it can last a long time and your investment will only suffer.

TREND #6. PATH OF PROGRESS

Path Moving Toward You

Recommendation for Single-Family Homes: Buy or Hold

Qualifications/Reasoning/Comments: The path of progress is often determined early on in a city's development and continues for decades. If you're ahead of the path, you want to buy as early as possible and hold until the path reaches you and the area is fully developed.

Path Moving Away from You

Recommendation for Single-Family Homes: Sell

Qualifications/Reasoning/Comments: When the path has reached you and your area is becoming fully developed, it's time to consider selling. Don't wait too long trying to squeeze out the last nickel; let the buyer make some money too. Although it doesn't happen often, the path of progress can change direction. If it changes before it reaches your area, you want to sell immediately.

TREND #7. NEW CONSTRUCTION

Equal to or Less Than Demand

Recommendation for Single-Family Homes: Buy or Hold

Qualifications/Reasoning/Comments: The actual amount of new construction doesn't matter much, as long as it's not greater than the demand. The more the new construction falls short of demand, the more it's a signal to buy. You do need to watch new construction, though, because if demand drops off, it may leave a lot of new supply in an environment of lower demand.

Greater Than Demand

Recommendation for Single-Family Homes: Sell

Qualifications/Reasoning/Comments: If new construction is dramatically higher than demand, it's a signal to sell. Matching supply and demand is not an exact science. It's common for construction to be a little more or a little less than demand. Don't be concerned with short-term, relatively small inequalities. It's the big differences you need to look for.

Timing Recommendations for Apartments

Apartment properties can vary from duplexes (two apartment units) to properties with over 1,000 units. Regardless of size, the seven trends generally affect most apartment properties in similar ways. A unique factor with apartments is the fact that they compete with single-family homes for consumer demand. For instance, apartments are usually the next choice for those who can't afford single-family homes.

TREND #1. INFLATION

Moderate (1% to 10%)

Recommendation for Apartment Buildings: Buy, Sell, or Hold

Qualifications/Reasoning/Comments: This level of inflation has a neutral influence on apartments. Decisions should be based on personal needs and other market conditions.

Hyperinflation (>10%)

Recommendation for Apartment Buildings: Sell

Qualifications/Reasoning/Comments: Hyperinflation is often a negative for apartments, especially in the near term. Costs can rise rapidly, but you can usually increase rental rates only every six months to one year. As a result, revenues won't keep pace with rising expenses, resulting in NOI moving up more slowly than inflation or even falling.

Deflation (<0%)

Recommendation for Apartment Buildings: Sell

Qualifications/Reasoning/Comments: Deflation is not good for apartments. Price wars with other apartments would require special promotions, e.g., free rent. A brief period of deflation, a year or even 18 months, is not a disaster. But multiple years of deflation can be devastating for most real estate.

TREND #2. INTEREST RATES

Low to Moderate (5%-10%)

Recommendation for Apartment Buildings: Buy, Sell, or Hold

Qualifications/Reasoning/Comments: This level of interest rate is favorable for buying, selling, or holding. However, extremely low interest rates should make you begin to think about selling. If you choose to hold instead, you would want to lock in the longest-term fixed-rate mortgage possible at the lowest interest rate possible. Then you won't be hurt when interest rates begin to rise. A factor specific to apartments is that when interest rates are low or declining, purchasing a home becomes an affordable option for a lot of renters. Consequently, apartments will be hurt as renters who qualify vacate apartments and buy homes.

High (>10%)

Recommendation for Apartment Buildings: Hold or Sell

Qualifications/Reasoning/Comments: Periods of high interest rates are generally not good times for buying. As with single-family homes, selling is a good option if you have an assumable loan at a lower interest rate, giving the purchaser a reason to pay a premium for the property at the lower rate.

TREND #3. FLOW OF FUNDS

Flow In

Recommendation for Apartment Buildings: Buy or Hold

Qualifications/Reasoning/Comments: When money is flowing into apartments, you want to be buying or holding. In 1981, for instance, the new tax law gave very favorable tax treatment to real estate and caused a huge inflow of money into apartments. (However, be careful not to hold too long.)

Flow Out

Recommendation for Apartment Buildings: Sell or Hold

Qualifications/Reasoning/Comments: When money is beginning to flow out of apartments, you want to sell. In 1986, when the tax law changed, even though prices already had started down, selling was still the smart move. However, if it's late in the cycle, prices have most likely already declined significantly, so you should hold.

TREND #4. JOB GROWTH

Steady or Increasing

Recommendation for Apartment Buildings: Buy or Hold

Qualifications/Reasoning/Comments: Steady or increasing job growth is good for apartments. Many people who come to a city for a new job at least initially will rent an apartment until they get settled. Those who cannot afford a home or don't want to own will continue to rent.

Negative or Rapid Decline

Recommendation for Apartment Buildings: Sell

Qualifications/Reasoning/Comments: When a market is experiencing a loss of jobs, it's typically a good time to sell. Renters will walk away from a lease far more readily than homeowners will walk away from a home. This is detrimental to the apartment owner who has to replace the renter: you lose revenues and you incur costs to clean and repair the apartment for the next tenant. Often in such an environment, in addition to losing the tenant, the owner will have to rent that apartment at a lower rent than previously in order to compete for the smaller number of renters.

TREND #5. MIGRATION

Into the Area

Recommendation for Apartment Buildings: Buy or Hold

Qualifications/Reasoning/Comments: There are always new apartments being added to the supply, even in down times, so people must be moving into an area just to keep pace with increasing supply. As an apartment owner, you want the newcomers to have low or moderate incomes, because people with higher incomes almost certainly will buy homes.

Out of the Area

Recommendation for Apartment Buildings: Sell

Qualifications/Reasoning/Comments: When people start leaving the area, sell immediately. Net out-migration is never good and can become a permanent negative trend. If people leave the area, demand for apartments declines, possibly for an extended period of time. People who decide to leave town often break their leases, causing a negative economic spiral for apartment owners.

TREND #6. PATH OF PROGRESS

Path Moving Toward You

Recommendation for Apartment Buildings: Buy or Hold

Qualifications/Reasoning/Comments: Apartments depend on high occupancy to cover all of the fixed costs of ownership, so it's not wise to buy far ahead of the path of progress. You cannot afford to wait for years for enough people to want to rent from you. If you are in the near-term path of progress, you will want to buy and hold until the development is complete in your area.

Path Moving Away from You

Recommendation for Apartment Buildings: Sell or Hold

Qualifications/Reasoning/Comments: It's less important to sell if the path of progress hits your area and continues on than if it moves away from your property. This is because as long as there is sufficient demand for your apartments, your operations can be strong.

However, the new hot spot would increase in value more quickly, so if you "think like a trader," you should consider selling a property when its price peaks and buy another one in the new path of progress.

TREND #7. NEW CONSTRUCTION

Equal to or Less Than Demand

Recommendation for Apartment Buildings: Buy or Hold

Qualifications/Reasoning/Comments: This is good news for apartment owners. When construction isn't keeping pace with demand, you typically can raise rents. It's a great time to buy apartments or hold the ones you already have.

Greater Than Demand

Recommendation for Apartment Buildings: Sell or Hold

Qualifications/Reasoning/Comments: If new construction is dramatically higher than demand, this is a signal to sell. Historically, apartments have experienced periods of such intense overbuilding that many years were required for an area to fully recover. If overbuilding is moderate, consider holding.

Timing Recommendations for Raw Land

Raw land as a real estate investment is unique, because it does not typically generate income. Based on property taxes, interest on mortgage debt, and other miscellaneous expenditures, land prices may have to go up roughly 10% per year to break even. This puts a lot of pressure on knowing where future growth will be.

TREND #1. INFLATION

Moderate (1% to 10%)

Recommendation for Raw Land: Buy, Sell, or Hold

Qualifications/Reasoning/Comments: Inflation will have a generally positive upward pressure on land prices, in much the same way that it puts upward pressure on other types of real estate.

Hyperinflation (>10%)

Recommendation for Raw Land: Hold or Sell

Qualifications/Reasoning/Comments: Land has rather limited costs (usually just a mortgage, taxes, and perhaps a little maintenance, such as mowing). Even extremely high inflation really is not a big negative. Land often continues to appreciate during hyperinflation.

Deflation (<0%)

Recommendation for Raw Land: Sell

Qualifications/Reasoning/Comments: Deflation puts downward pressure on prices for all types of real estate, including raw land.

TREND #2. INTEREST RATES

Low to Moderate (5%-10%)

Recommendation for Raw Land: Buy, Sell, or Hold

Qualifications/Reasoning/Comments: Moderate interest rates are a sign of stability. They're good for land values, because land values depend upon economic stability.

High (>10%)

Recommendation for Raw Land: Hold or Sell

Qualifications/Reasoning/Comments: High interest rates make it harder to sell land. Mortgage payments for a new buyer will be higher, unless a buyer is willing to pay cash. However, land prices will not necessarily fall if interest rates are high, because land prices depend more on the investor's belief in the growth of an area than in interest rates or inflation.

TREND #3. FLOW OF FUNDS

Flow In

Recommendation for Raw Land: Buy or Hold

Qualifications/Reasoning/Comments: You should buy when money begins to flow in and hold while money is flowing in, but sell at the first sign that the trend is turning.

Flow Out

Recommendation for Raw Land: Sell or Hold

If you wait until the trend is well established, you'll need to wait for the next cycle.

TREND #4. JOB GROWTH

Steady or Increasing

Recommendation for Raw Land: Buy or Hold

Qualifications/Reasoning/Comments: Job growth is a key factor in land prices, particularly if the land is located in an undeveloped or under-developed area.

Negative or Rapid Decline

Recommendation for Raw Land: Sell

Qualifications/Reasoning/Comments: If job growth slows or there are losses, land prices would be severely impacted. Prices for land will move with the perception of how soon the land could be developed successfully.

TREND #5. MIGRATION

Into the Area

Recommendation for Raw Land: Buy or Hold

Qualifications/Reasoning/Comments: Migration into the area is always a positive for land value. Like job growth, this tells prospective buyers that this land is likely to be put to productive use in the near future.

Out of the Area

Recommendation for Raw Land: Sell

Qualifications/Reasoning/Comments: Migration out of an area would have an even more negative impact on land value than would job loss.

TREND #6. PATH OF PROGRESS

Path Moving Toward You

Recommendation for Raw Land: Buy or Hold

Qualifications/Reasoning/Comments: If any single real estate type is most dramatically impacted by the path of progress, I would say it's land. Land that is not in the path of progress or that is well ahead of the path of progress usually can be bought cheaply. However, prices rise quickly and dramatically when the land is in demand for development. Because buying land has fewer fixed costs than other types of real estate, you can afford to buy raw land a little more ahead of the path of progress and get a better price, which provides for much greater upside potential.

Path Moving Away from You

Recommendation for Raw Land: Sell

Qualifications/Reasoning/Comments: If it becomes clear that the path of progress is moving away from you, sell immediately. Land that is not in the path of progress may not be developed for many, many years. You don't want to hold land that is not appreciating for decades. Put your money to better use.

TREND #7. NEW CONSTRUCTION

Equal to or Less Than Demand

Recommendation for Raw Land: Buy, Hold, or Sell

Qualifications/Reasoning/Comments: Prices for land in the middle of nowhere, where there is no construction, are not going to dramatically increase.

Greater Than Demand

Recommendation for Raw Land: Buy, Hold, or Sell

Qualifications/Reasoning/Comments: Land prices spike when there's a critical mass of development in the area that makes everyone else want to start building there as well. This is why all new construction may be good for raw land even if it is projected to exceed demand in the near term.

Timing Recommendations for Office Property

Though office property doesn't behave exactly like other commercial real estate investments, there are many parallels in how the seven trends affect transaction timing for all types of commercial property.

TREND #1. INFLATION

Moderate (1% to 10%)

Recommendation for Office Property: Buy, Sell, or Hold

Qualifications/Reasoning/Comments: This level of inflation has a neutral influence on office buildings. Decisions should depend on personal needs and other market conditions.

Hyperinflation (>10%)

Recommendation for Office Property: Hold or Sell

Qualifications/Reasoning/Comments: Hyperinflation can impact expenses of office properties in a way similar to apartments if you don't pass the expense increase on to tenants. With office properties, you often must wait even longer than with apartments before you can raise rents (typically five to 10 years). This makes it difficult for an owner to improve NOI and catch up with inflation.

Deflation (<0%)

Recommendation for Office Property: Sell or Hold

Qualifications/Reasoning/Comments: Deflation is not good for office properties. However, for the same reason that you can't raise rents rapidly, namely long-term leases, your rents won't fall rapidly either. This will give you time to arrange a sale. In fact, lower expenses, in the short term, could make your NOI briefly higher. If you believe the deflation will be short term, a year or less, then a hold strategy is recommended; otherwise, sell.

TREND #2. INTEREST RATES

Low to Moderate (5%-10%)

Recommendation for Office Property: Buy, Sell, or Hold

Qualifications/Reasoning/Comments: Low to moderate interest rates are favorable for buying, selling, or holding. However, extremely low interest rates are a sign to sell. It's better to get the advantage of higher prices when rates are low. If you choose to hold instead, you would want to lock in the longest-term fixed-rate mortgage you can get at the low point in the trend. Then you won't be hurt when interest rates begin to rise again.

High (>10%)

Recommendation for Office Property: Hold or Sell

Qualifications/Reasoning/Comments: Office buildings are usually a pricey investment. High interest rates can make holding onto office property expensive. For this reason, if you want to sell, you need to do so as soon as you see marked increases in interest rates. Don't wait for them to get too high. When rates get higher, your market of buyers evaporates because it's difficult for them to find financing.

TREND #3. FLOW OF FUNDS

Flow In

Recommendation for Office Property: Buy or Hold

Qualifications/Reasoning/Comments: You want to buy when money starts flowing into office buildings. You would hold while money is flowing in.

Flow Out

Recommendation for Office Property: Sell or Hold

Qualifications/Reasoning/Comments: If you wait until well into the time that money is flowing out of office buildings, you may need to wait for the next cycle.

TREND #4. JOB GROWTH

Steady or Increasing

Recommendation for Office Property: Buy or Hold

Qualifications/Reasoning/Comments: Steady or increasing job growth is even more crucial for office buildings than for other types of real estate. Office buildings depend on tenants, who only grow and need more space when they are adding employees.

Negative or Rapid Decline

Recommendation for Office Property: Sell

Qualifications/Reasoning/Comments: If job growth becomes negative, meaning a loss of jobs, this typically is a signal to sell. When businesses cut employees, tenants also cut back on their lease space. As owners usually require long-term leases, tenants can't cut back immediately, but often, if the decline continues, tenants default on rent or go bankrupt. They also begin to sublease their space to other tenants, which further hurts owners by taking companies off the market that would have rented new space.

TREND #5. MIGRATION

Into the Area

Recommendation for Office Property: Buy or Hold

Qualifications/Reasoning/Comments: New people migrating to your area are extremely important for office buildings. Companies generally locate close to their employment base. Therefore, the more well-educated prospective employees who live in an area, the more companies will want to move to that area.

Out of the Area

Recommendation for Office Property: Sell

Qualifications/Reasoning/Comments: When people start leaving the area, sell immediately. It may take some time because of existing leases, but if large numbers of any company's employees move to another area or if another area has much better prospective employees, a company will relocate to be closer to the workers it wants to attract.

TREND #6. PATH OF PROGRESS

Path Moving Toward You

Recommendation for Office Property: Buy or Hold

Qualifications/Reasoning/Comments: Office buildings are high-cost operations. You can't afford to wait for years for enough people to want to lease office space in your building. But being out ahead of the path of progress allows you to buy at a more favorable price than when the path of development reaches your area.

Path Moving Away from You

Recommendation for Office Property: Sell or Hold

Qualifications/Reasoning/Comments: If it becomes clear that the path of progress is moving away from you, evaluate how it will hurt your property. Is your office building still in a highly desirable area? If not, either sell immediately or plan a holding strategy and adjust your expectations.

TREND #7. NEW CONSTRUCTION

Equal to or Less Than Demand

Recommendation for Office Property: Buy or Hold

Qualifications/Reasoning/Comments: Office buildings take longer to build than most other types of real estate. It can take from two to five years to plan and build a major project. As a result, it is somewhat easier to see ahead of time how much space is going to come on line. If a small amount of space is coming on line in the future while demand is above this level, prices will rise and you will want to buy or hold.

Greater Than Demand

Recommendation for Office Property: Sell

Qualifications/Reasoning/Comments: If new construction is dramatically higher than demand, it's time to sell. More than any other type of real estate, office buildings have become seriously overbuilt at various times, because of the long timeline to plan and build them. New projects, begun when demand seems strong, often miss the mark by the time construction is completed. If you are building office properties, there is little you can do. But, if you have buildings now, you can watch these supply-demand dynamics and react accordingly before the market is seriously overbuilt.

Timing Recommendations for Retail

Within the retail real estate classification, there is a wide range of product types, from single specialty stores to large shopping malls. For the purposes of this discussion, we will take a broad-brush look at retail in general.

TREND #1. INFLATION

Moderate (1% to 10%)

Recommendation for Retail Property: Buy, Sell, or Hold

Qualifications/Reasoning/Comments: This level of inflation has a neutral influence on retail. Decisions should depend upon your personal needs and other market conditions.

Hyperinflation (>10%)

Recommendation for Retail Property: Hold or Sell

Qualifications/Reasoning/Comments: Like office leases, retail leases are usually several years long, and you can increase rents only as leases expire. To a degree, you can offset your own rising costs with expense escalators, but you can only pass along a set maximum expense increase according to your lease terms.

Deflation (<0%)

Recommendation for Retail Property: Sell or Hold

Qualifications/Reasoning/Comments: Retail can be hurt even worse than office properties during times of deflation. You want to sell if you sense any long-term move toward deflation.

TREND #2. INTEREST RATES

Low to Moderate (5%–10%)

Recommendation for Retail Property: Buy, Sell, or Hold

Qualifications/Reasoning/Comments: This level of interest rate is favorable for buying, selling, or holding. Low interest rates are good for retail. As a general statement, retail does well in a low interest rate environment because it makes credit buying less burdensome. Therefore, owners of retail buildings do well, as do the retail stores.

High (>10%)

Recommendation for Retail Property: Hold or Sell

Qualifications/Reasoning/Comments: High interest rates make it harder for consumers to spend. This causes a pullback in spending, which hurts retail stores. The more poorly their sales go, the higher the probability that they move out or default on their rent.

TREND #3. FLOW OF FUNDS

Flow In

Recommendation for Retail Property: Buy or Hold

Qualifications/Reasoning/Comments: When money begins to flow into retail property, you should buy and hold.

Flow Out

Recommendation for Retail Property: Sell or Hold

Qualifications/Reasoning/Comments: When money first begins to flow out of retail, it's time to sell. If you wait until the trend is fully developed, you'll need to wait for the next cycle.

TREND #4. JOB GROWTH

Steady or Increasing

Recommendation for Retail Property: Buy or Hold

Qualifications/Reasoning/Comments: Job growth drives consumer spending. When people have solid jobs and feel secure, they spend freely. Steady positive or increasing job growth is an accurate predictor of rising retail real estate prices.

Negative or Rapid Decline

Recommendation for Retail Property: Sell

Qualifications/Reasoning/Comments: If job growth sours, it's a signal to sell. Retail sales and the associated health of retail tenants depend on job growth.

TREND #5. MIGRATION

Into the Area

Recommendation for Retail Property: Buy or Hold

Qualifications/Reasoning/Comments: Migration into an area dramatically improves the value of retail real estate. Retail is an extremely local product. People tend to shop close to their homes, so you should carefully watch population growth figures for areas in which you're thinking about buying retail real estate. The ones with steady growth or, preferably, rising rates of growth are the areas in which to buy.

Out of the Area

Recommendation for Retail Property: Sell

Qualifications/Reasoning/Comments: When people start moving away from an area, sell immediately. The success of retail depends closely on the number of "rooftops" near it. Most national retail chains will not build without a set number of homeowners in the area. They'll use these same numbers as criteria to close a location if too many people move out of an area. The prices for retail properties will drop quickly and dramatically when buyers realize that consumers are moving to other areas.

TREND #6. PATH OF PROGRESS

Path Moving Toward You

Recommendation for Retail Property: Buy or Hold

Qualifications/Reasoning/Comments: The most dramatic increases in the price of retail real estate occur when people realize that an area is starting to boom. The best way to make money is to spot the boom area ahead of time and buy.

Path Moving Away from You

Recommendation for Retail Property: Sell or Hold

Qualifications/Reasoning/Comments: If it becomes clear that the path of progress is moving away from you, sell immediately.

Trend #7. New Construction

Equal to or Less Than Demand

Recommendation for Retail Property: Buy or Hold

Qualifications/Reasoning/Comments: Buying when new construction is less than demand is often a successful strategy. But there are several factors that make this more difficult in retail than with other types of real estate. First, retail has a fairly short construction timeline. Second, today retail is often developed in large projects, as opposed to smaller neighborhood centers. And third, retail has a "pack mentality," meaning many retail centers are built at the same time.

Greater Than Demand

Recommendation for Retail Property: Sell

Qualifications/Reasoning/Comments: You need to keep a close eye on new construction. Because a flood of it can come in a rush, you want to be ready to sell quickly if you see excess construction. If you fail to see the flood coming, it likely will be too late to sell when the flood arrives, because prices for existing retail property will have fallen already to compete with the huge amount of new supply. The only mitigating factor that should make you consider holding instead of selling is if the area is growing rapidly enough to absorb the supply in relatively short order.

Timing Recommendations for Hospitality—Hotels and Motels

Hotels and motels have some advantages over other types of real estate in tough times, because long-term leases don't bind them. The most unique aspect of the hospitality sector compared with other real estate is that it is far more operations-intensive. In many ways, hotels and motels are a combination of real estate and commercial business.

TREND #1. INFLATION

Moderate (1% to 10%)

Recommendation for Hotels/Motels: Buy, Sell, or Hold

Qualifications/Reasoning/Comments: This level of inflation has a neutral influence on product. Decisions should depend upon personal needs and on other market conditions.

Hyperinflation (>10%)

Recommendation for Hotels/Motels: Hold or Sell

Qualifications/Reasoning/Comments: Hotels and motels have the ability to adjust rental rates daily, so there is less pressure to sell in an inflationary environment than with some other types of real estate. However, hyperinflation is an unstable economic condition and many other negative things can happen, such as job loss and out-migration.

Deflation (<0%)

Recommendation for Hotels/Motels: Sell

Qualifications/Reasoning/Comments: The ability to change rates daily is a negative here, as opposed to being a positive in the high-inflation environment. Guests will insist on lower and lower prices while many expenses remain fixed, causing value to drop.

TREND #2. INTEREST RATES

Low to Moderate (5%-10%)

Recommendation for Hotels/Motels: Buy, Sell, or Hold

Qualifications/Reasoning/Comments: Hotels do well in stable economic environments, so this level of interest rate is favorable for buying, selling, or holding.

High (>10%)

Recommendation for Hotels/Motels: Hold or Sell

Qualifications/Reasoning/Comments: High interest rates are bad for hotels, especially if you need to take on any new debt for rehabilitation or other major expenses. High interest rates also would have negative effects if a hotel owner's mortgage matures when rates are high. If, however, the hotel had a mortgage assumable at a significantly lower interest rate, this would make it desirable for a purchaser to buy the property.

TREND #3. FLOW OF FUNDS

Flow In

Recommendation for Hotels/Motels: Buy or Hold

Qualifications/Reasoning/Comments: You should buy when money begins to flow in and hold while money is flowing in, but don't wait too long. If funds have been flowing into hotels for some time, sell early to be safe.

Flow Out

Recommendation for Hotels/Motels: Sell or Hold

Qualifications/Reasoning/Comments: Sell early in the trend. If you wait until the trend is established, you may need to hold until the next cycle.

TREND #4. JOB GROWTH

Steady or Increasing

Recommendation for Hotels/Motels: Buy or Hold

Qualifications/Reasoning/Comments: Hotels and motels get their guests from pleasure and business travelers. A significant number of business guests come from local businesses that bring people in from out of town; therefore, hotels need local businesses to be growing and doing well to generate business travel.

Negative or Rapid Decline

Recommendation for Hotels/Motels: Sell or Hold

Qualifications/Reasoning/Comments: If job growth slows or there is a loss of jobs, it's a signal to look carefully at the market and evaluate selling versus holding. Companies are quick to cut back on business travel expenses if they aren't making their numbers. If you see a company cutting back on jobs, it probably already has cut back on business travel.

TREND #5. MIGRATION

Into the Area

Recommendation for Hotels/Motels: Buy or Hold

Qualifications/Reasoning/Comments: Migration into the area is always a positive, but it has less impact on hotels than on most other types of real estate. That's because the pleasure travelers for hotels usually come from outside the area. Relatively few residents in the area stay at local hotels. If they do, it is typically for an isolated, special purpose.

Out of the Area

Recommendation for Hotels/Motels: Sell

Qualifications/Reasoning/Comments: Likewise, out-migration, although a negative, has less direct impact on hotels. There would still be the indirect impact, because if people are moving out of the area, the local businesses are losing employees, which in turn could cause them to cut back on business travel.

TREND #6. PATH OF PROGRESS

Path Moving Toward You

Recommendation for Hotels/Motels: Buy or Hold

Qualifications/Reasoning/Comments: If you can find a hotel that is in the path of progress but nobody has recognized it as such, you can do well with the investment. As development continues around the hotel, you would benefit by the new support retail and office space.

Path Moving Away from You

Recommendation for Hotels/Motels: Sell or Hold

Qualifications/Reasoning/Comments: If it becomes clear that the path of progress is moving away from you, sell immediately. Hotels will lose value once buyers realize that the area is no longer hot.

TREND #7. NEW CONSTRUCTION

Equal to or Less Than Demand

Recommendation for Hotels/Motels: Buy or Hold

Qualifications/Reasoning/Comments: Similar to office buildings, hotels have a long timeline from design to completion. This should allow you to spot when demand is going to be greater than supply.

Greater Than Demand

Recommendation for Hotels/Motels: Sell

Qualifications/Reasoning/Comments: This lag time should also provide some advance warning about when to sell. The wildcard to consider is exogenous shocks (discussed later in this chapter), such as the tragedy of 9/11, which hurt hotel prices dramatically even in markets where demand previously had been greater than supply, because demand declined deeply and immediately.

Trends in Action

So far I've discussed each trend as if it were alone in impacting your buy, sell, or hold timing decision. The reality is that the seven trends don't happen alone. Instead, the relationships among the trends become an important element in timing.

The seven trends don't happen alone. Instead, the relationships among the trends become an important element in timing.

Yet, typically, you will find dominating trends in any given cycle. For example, the dominant trend in 1983, 1984, and 1985 was too much construction. In many cycles, once one trend turns negative, others reinforce it, turning a bad situation worse overnight. In 1983 and 1984, it seemed to most investors that inflation was going to be rising continuously. High interest rates weren't a problem because of higher inflation and investors seemed to fall all over themselves chasing higher prices for properties. Moreover, the flow of funds was positive because of the 1981 tax law.

By 1986, the oversupply from new construction was evident. The tax law had changed, cutting off a huge flow of funds, and inflation turned decisively downward with oil prices plummeting. A combination of all of these trends began to reinforce a downward cycle.

There are also times when trends move in opposite directions and keep the market more or less neutral. But more often than not, it seems that cycles are extended and made deeper and more severe by a combination of trends occurring at the same time. Usually, success breeds success on the upside and failure breeds failure on the downside.

Ironically, I believe, and I hope I can convince you as an investor to believe, that the safest and best course is to buy at the bottom of a cycle. I say "ironically" because most people simply are afraid to buy when prices are low, fearing the negative trends that produce depressed prices will continue indefinitely. No one knows with certainty when these negative trends have bottomed out and, even with the best analytical tools, no one can scientifically identify the top or bottom of any market cycle. But the important point here is that it's still far safer to buy when you think you're near the bottom and then sell too early as opposed to waiting until it's too late to sell.

The safest and best course is to buy at the bottom of a cycle.

It seems obvious that this is a safer way to approach real estate investing, but it's never easy to spend large amounts of money at the bottom of a cycle, when your emotions and your friends may be telling you you're crazy. But over my 35-year career, this has been the key to my most successful real estate investments.

The Wildcard—Exogenous Shocks

Don't be frightened by the strange title. "Exogenous shocks" is a term often used in economics to describe extreme or out-of-the ordinary events. To the extent that economics has predictable patterns that can be understood scientifically, exogenous shocks throw off the patterns.

An extreme example of an exogenous shock with which we are all familiar is the September 11, 2001 terrorist attack. That unexpected event dramatically changed economic activities. Office, retail, and apartment space in and around the World Trade Center plummeted in value. Hotels nationally suffered due to the dramatic decline in airline traffic and leisure travel. The effect of this one unexpected event was felt in all segments of the economy.

Another example is the Iraq War. Maybe as economically important as the war itself was the period of uncertainty for months before the war. Lower consumer and investor confidence caused a stagnation in the business cycle. It affected investors' confidence and the resulting uncertainty, in turn, impacted real estate and other investments adversely.

Exogenous shocks, however, can provide opportunities to buy when prices are deeply discounted. While you can't predict them, you can react to them and capitalize on them if you stay in tune. For example, in the next chapter I discuss a hotel that we purchased and renovated in 2002. Part of the reason we were able to buy the property at a great price was due to operational difficulties that were exacerbated by a large decline in business travel after 9/11.

Using the Seven Trends in the Real World

Real estate cycles have four basic stages. The first stage is the up cycle, when property prices are rising. The second stage is the plateau, when prices are stabilized at a high point. The plateau stage can vary in duration from a brief moment in time to an extended period. When the plateau stage ends, the third stage—the down cycle—begins. The end of the down cycle signals the fourth and final stage, which is the bottom. Like the plateau at the top of the cycle, the bottom is characterized by stabilized prices and can be very brief.

These cycles are at the heart of understanding timing in the real estate market. By being aware of these cycles and seeing their relationship with the seven trends, you greatly improve your chances of being a successful real estate investor.

Real estate cycles vary greatly. They differ in terms of length, degree, and intensity. History generally has shown us that most, though not all, real estate cycles have longer and higher upsides than downsides. This means that, over time, prices of properties continue a long-term upward trend, even though cycles can be violent and unforgiving in the short run.

Understanding Trend Interaction

Real estate is highly cyclical and a local phenomenon. Prices vary based on property type and the seven major trends. Within cycles, each of the seven trends moves at its own pace. These movements sometime reinforce each other to cause increased momentum in one direction or another. Sometimes they actually contradict each other, making the overall real estate cycle more difficult to analyze.

Within cycles, each of the seven trends moves at its own pace. These movements sometime reinforce each other. Sometimes they actually contradict each other.

For example, when interest rates are going down, property prices are usually going up. But what if factors driving interest rates down are a depressed national economy and negative job growth? Negative job growth as discussed in Chapter 5 usually drives real estate prices down.

Counterbalanced trends such as these are not unusual. What becomes important in considering these counterbalances is the relative significance of the various trends within any given cycle.

Even in our world of formulas and predictive measurement, there are no simple rules ranking the significance of each of the major trends at precisely the moment we care to have the information. There are times when inflation, interest rates, job creation, or any combination of the trends can be more or less important to a specific type of property in a specific location.

If understanding trend interaction were easy, everyone would succeed and we would have a perfectly efficient marketplace, free of trial and error with little room for opportunity and profit. That is not what occurs. The more you know about the trends and understand how they work, the closer you get to identifying cycle direction. Simply being aware that there are trends at all allows you to take advantage of the real estate market trading arena's inefficiencies and promotes the possibility that you will succeed with your real estate investments.

> Even in our world of formulas and predictive measurement, there are no simple rules ranking the significance of each of the major trends.

Looking for Anecdotal Evidence

No matter what your business is, you need a basic knowledge of all the factors that can impact your success. Having a fundamental understanding of the seven major trends that impact real estate is a basic necessity for real estate investing success.

Likewise, hearing opinions on the state of the market from people who are in the business is key—not only to enhance your knowledge and understanding, but also to stay on top of current trends and the psychology of the marketplace. Talking with real estate professionals, brokers, owners, managers, and others is crucial. Anecdotal evidence about whether prices are going up or down is fairly easy to get. The key is to figure out how to plot the cycle data you obtain, i.e., do the prices indicate early, mid, or late points in the cycle? Usually you can determine where you are in a cycle through your own logic and common sense coupled with a basic knowledge of the seven major trends. Further, you should know what trends in particular are affecting the different types of property in your market area of interest.

Remember that none of your conclusions will be precise or permanent. You will need to place greater or lesser degrees of importance on any one area at different times along the way.

Pulling It All Together

The best way to pull it all together to identify where your property stands in the cycle is to combine your analyses of each of the seven major trends with anecdotal local market research, meaning what you've learned from talking with others about prices in the marketplace. By listening to others in the business, hopefully you've received opinions on where cap rates are going. You've learned what is happening in the local area and why. For example, if you are considering buying single-family houses to rent, you have talked with brokers who normally sell that kind of real estate. You have looked at local MLS data to find out what's been happening to the prices of similar properties. From all this it's not hard to get a strong gut feeling for which direction your property is likely to head. If you compare this information with the information plotted for each of the seven trends, you'll see more clearly where your property stands in the cycle.

By creating simple graphs, you can plot the trends for yourself. You can note where you think your property is in relation to the rest of the market.

For example, let's pretend that it's early 2003 and we want to see where prices of apartments are likely headed in Dallas, Texas. For this purpose, let's take a look at Figure 7-1.

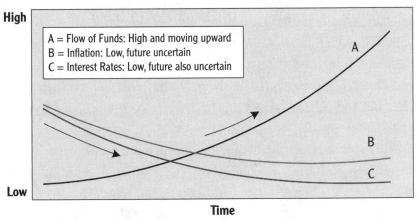

Figure 7-1. Dallas apartment buildings, national trends as of early 2003

Here we can see the impact of the three national trends as they might impact apartment pricing in Dallas. We also find that inflation and interest rates are both difficult to predict. While inflation has been coming down, which generally might be a slight negative for prices, it is difficult to predict which direction it is heading from this point forward. Inflation could be turning to deflation, which might be a big negative, or we could be bottoming out and about to start a new inflationary cycle, which would be a big positive. It is simply uncertain. Likewise, interest rates have come down, may be bottoming out, and may be ready to start up again, which would be a negative. If we're buying a new apartment building and can finance it at today's current low rates, then the overall national interest rate situation is a positive. Ironically, even the fact that rates might be headed upward could be a positive, if we have already financed our property before that happens. Finally, the third of the national trends, flow of funds: huge amounts of money continue to move into real estate. To the extent that this continues, pricing should be positively affected, as cap rates will be driven downward.

Now let's look at Figure 7-2, which relates to the four local trends. Here we see that new construction, even though slowing, remains far higher than current demand. As a result, we have had and continue to have increasing vacancies. This is a negative for current and near-term net operating income. Similarly, job growth is declining, which is an additional huge negative for NOI. Migration and path of progress, for the purposes of this example, are both neutral. Overall, the local trends show us that NOI has recently been declining and will likely continue to decline. Declining NOI, all things being equal, usually means declining prices.

This specific example highlights the current confusing cycle. It is not unusual for trends to conflict with each other. When it happens, you have to decide which is the most dominant trend. However, what has happened with apartment prices in early 2003 is repeated in virtually every other property sector and throughout most markets in

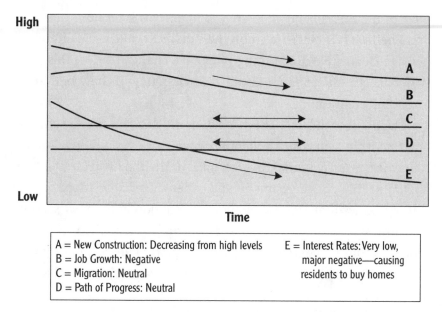

A = New Construction: Decreasing from high levels
B = Job Growth: Negative
C = Migration: Neutral
D = Path of Progress: Neutral

E = Interest Rates: Very low, major negative—causing residents to buy homes

Figure 7-2. Dallas apartment buildings, local trends as of early 2003

the U.S. NOI is going down, which usually would mean prices go down. But what is happening is that cap rates are going down even faster and prices generally have been stable to higher. The primary reason for this is flow of funds. There is simply so much money coming into the real estate markets that, even despite current trends that would suggest lower prices, we are likely to see price stability or even higher prices going forward.

One of the first questions that arise from this example is "How long will the flow of funds trend dominate over other trends that are more specific to net operating results?" The next question to consider is "How long will net operating results continue in a downward trend or are we at or near the bottom in negative job creation, excessive new construction, and so on?" These are two key examples of the kind of thought processes and judgments that you must make to time the market.

My own analysis of the Dallas apartment market in 2003 is that, unless you are buying with a new, very low interest rate mortgage, most of the prices being paid are too high. This is an uncertain time and I believe it is better to sit on the sidelines while cycle directions become clearer. No doubt things will have changed before this book is published. My opinions could also change with new and additional information.

The point of this discussion is not as much about the specifics on apartments in Dallas as it is about the ways of considering and plotting where your potential investment is at the time you are thinking about making the investment and where it's likely to be in the future. Rather than use a hypothetical situation in the next section, let's discuss a real-world example that includes the entire process my real estate investment company uses to plot where a property is in the cycle and then decide whether or not it would be a good acquisition for us.

A Real-World Example: Radisson Hotel DFW South, Dallas 2002

Real-world experiences help paint historical pictures on which future plans can be based. What follows is one such example of a recent Hall Financial Group acquisition and the process we used to make a series of critical decisions.

Our investing approach has always been contrarian, and it was in keeping with this strategy that we began to analyze the Dallas hospitality market. We wanted to find a property to hold for a period of three to 10 years. We reviewed opportunities, looking for matches to our buying criteria, and found one situation that was particularly compelling. In March of 2002, we purchased a Wilson World Hotel that was operating poorly and in need of significant capital improvements. In conjunction with making the important physical upgrades, we chose to rebrand the hotel and operate it under the Radisson flag.

Here's the five-step process we used to analyze this particular property:

Using the Seven Trends in the Real World

1. Look at the seven trends.
2. Consider exogenous events.
3. Assess barriers to entry.
4. Review anecdotal evidence.
5. Pull it all together.

STEP #1. LOOK AT THE SEVEN TRENDS

National Trend #1: Inflation. It was our feeling that the current low inflation was a near-term neutral to a slight negative and a longer-term positive, because we believed that inflation would be higher in coming years. We also believed inflation would have little impact on the Dallas hotel market, both from the expense and the revenue sides. Replacement costs due to inflation likely would be negligible, as new construction rates, if any at all, were deflating. Moreover, due to the condition of the hotel market in Dallas, few if any new hotels were planned in most competitive submarkets. Inflation in general was a neutral factor, although with it came some near-term risk of deflation. Because of the overall economic circumstances and a tug-of-war between inflationary and deflationary sources, some potential risks of deflation merited consideration.

In the mid to longer term, we made the general assumption that the Federal Reserve was attempting to expand the money supply and that, ultimately, there was a lot of government pressure for fiscal stimulus. We believed that the monetary and fiscal stimulus ultimately would kick-start growth in the broader economy and result in an uptick in inflation down the line. This potentially would be a plus for hotels as well as other real estate, because hotels can raise rates on a daily basis. As a result, inflationary pressures from the marketplace could be passed along via instant changes in pricing structures. If a new competitive product eventually came on line because of increased occupancy levels and better pricing structures, the new product would have been built at inflated costs compared with our property.

National Trend #2: Interest Rates. Interest rates impact hotels in several ways, but none of them were extraordinarily significant to our 2002 considerations. Interest rates were quite low (a 1.25% Fed Funds rate), which is favorable for real estate, including hotels. While some hotels with floating rates had low interest rates of 3.5% to 4.5%, Wilson World had a higher fixed-rate mortgage of 9.2%, with seven years remaining. This high rate was certainly a negative for the hotel. To make matters worse, the current owners were unable to refinance at the prevailing lower rates because the property was underperforming. In general, even though interest rates were low, most lenders were being very conservative when considering making loans on hotels. In this sense, interest rates were less important than if the lending market for this property type were more active.

On an intermediate and longer-term basis, the interest rate situation was a bit of a negative. We believed rates over a five- to 10-year period were more likely to go up substantially, rather than staying at the current 1.25%. If Fed Funds increased to 6% or 7% by the time we were planning to sell, cap rates would be affected adversely hurting the value of the property.

National Trend #3: Flow of Funds. As I pointed out, mortgage loans for hotels in Dallas in 2002 were scarce. Similarly, there was an overall lack of equity. We thought this lack of money flowing into the hospitality market was a function of the current market alone and not a long-term situation.

Looking out over the intermediate to longer term and assuming no exogenous events, we projected an increase in new jobs created and other scenarios that would boost demand and increase occupancy rates and overall performance. We believed then and still do today that at some point in the next three to 10 years we will see this trigger a substantial increase of funds flowing into the market.

Taking all of these factors into account, we understood that the lack of fund flow to the real estate hospitality market sector was a major positive for us in buying the Wilson World Hotel because we could buy at a depressed price. As a contrarian investor, we normally buy when there is less money chasing the real estate in which we are interested.

Local Trend #1: Job Growth. Depending on the type of hotel property you are considering, both local and national job growth trends can make a difference. Local job growth has a positive impact on the overall vibrancy of the local market. However, for hotels, national job growth is more of an influencer for overall demand from business travelers.

From our investment perspective, nationally, non-farm employment fell dramatically, with a loss of 1,430,000 jobs in 2001 and an additional loss of 230,000 in 2002. These disastrous numbers followed many years of positive growth in the 1990s. Taken as a whole, negative job growth was one of the primary reasons many hotels performed poorly across the country.

In the mid to longer term, three to 10 years out, we felt job growth would improve in step with an overall improvement in the national economy. We believed local job growth in Dallas, which historically has been reflective of the national economy, would directly benefit from national job growth improvements. The recent telecommunications bust had a serious negative impact on Dallas employment. Job growth in the greater Dallas area in 2000 was 65,000, in 2001 it was a negative 62,000, and in 2002 it was a negative of 31,000. Again, we believed these numbers were less important than the national numbers, but they would have some impact because they indicated that local companies would not have as many business travelers coming into the market for meetings and conferences.

Considering all of the above, we viewed the job growth trend as a near-term negative but, related to our investment, as a major positive for our particular long-term strategy. While we could not know absolutely when negative job growth would turn around either nationally or locally, we believed it was at or near the bottom. We were confident there were better times ahead during the three- to 10-year period we planned to hold this property.

Local Trend #2: In- or Out-Migration. From our perspective, in- and out-migration would impact hotels as a property type moderately. While in- or out-migration is very important to residential and retail properties, both are less important to the office, industrial, and hotel sectors. Nevertheless, in the case of this hotel in 2002, net in-migration for Dallas was still positive even during the economic slowdown. Population increased in 2000 from 3,280,000 to 3,519,000 and then in 2001 to 3,646,000. For these reasons and for the purposes of our decision-making process, we considered this trend a slight positive.

Local Trend #3: Path of Progress. This particular property in Dallas is located right at the south exit to DFW International Airport. Like others, the airport has taken a hit from reduced overall air travel since 9/11. In the short run, what was clearly once in a path of progress anchored by a significant and growing airport now had stalled.

On the other hand, new construction inside DFW International Airport continued. A new international terminal and runways with a $1.1 billion price tag was in the works as part of a $2.6 billion capital improvement program. DFW currently serves 55 million travelers each year. With the new construction and expansion plans under way, it will eventually serve many more travelers. So, even though the current market was down, looking out over our planned holding period, we believed we will see positive things happening, especially where our hotel is located.

We viewed the path of progress trend for this purchase as a strong positive. From a timing perspective, we bought during a temporary lull or even a downturn relating to the path of progress trend. But it is evident that airport enhancements could increase dramatically the property's future value in three to 10 years.

Local Trend #4: New Construction. New construction in the hotel sector in Dallas was virtually nonexistent in 2002. This trend was due to lower hotel occupancies, lower rates, and generally poor operating results.

The new construction trend was a major positive to us. As is described more fully in the following steps, this factor will interact with the other trends in a way that we believe will help us during the holding period we have planned for this property.

STEP #2. CONSIDER EXOGENOUS EVENTS

Following 9/11, travel for both business and pleasure took a global downturn, seriously damaging the airline and travel industries worldwide. Even more than a year later, hotel occupancies remained down and many continued to perform poorly.

Also in 2002, the looming shadow of uncertainty associated with a potential war in Iraq only made matters worse. We were bombarded by the media with questions of "Will the U.S. invade or not?" and international travel moved further down on the priority list. With reduced demand, hotel NOI goes down. With future uncertainty, fund flow also goes down, as does the availability of investor capital. And cap rates remain higher than what might otherwise have been the case.

These exogenous events had an immediate negative impact, with certain lingering effects for the intermediate or longer term. We had to evaluate this risk carefully. In our view, terrorism and a war with Iraq are not the types of events that would affect the hotel adversely on a three- to 10-year basis. We ultimately chose to buy.

STEP #3. ASSESS BARRIERS TO ENTRY

One of the benefits of the then current lack of new construction in the hotel business was that, when hotels become more fashionable for new construction again, costs will have gone up. That will give the Radisson Hotel DFW South a more favorable market position and generally will bar entry into the market at a comparable price. This factor will increase our hotel's competitive advantage over hotels that are constructed three to 10 years from now.

STEP #4. REVIEW ANECDOTAL EVIDENCE

In terms of timing, the hotel industry appeared to us to be at or near a low point. Many companies involved in the business were suffering from multiple years of downturn. I'm a big believer in the saying, "It's darkest before the dawn." The fact is, when you are in the middle of tough times, it is hard to believe things will ever get better. But they do.

I'm a big believer in the saying, "It's darkest before the dawn."

The psychology of timing markets is easier to write about than it is to experience, especially when you're right in the middle of a difficult time. On the other hand, when the general consensus is gloomy, that could be a good sign for the contrarian timing investment approach we have found successful.

Being directly involved in the Dallas market, prior to our purchase, we had access to many bright business associates and acquaintances in the hospitality industry. They agreed that our plan to buy and renovate this hotel was based on sound fundamentals and it was likely that the Dallas-area hotel market would recover over the next few years.

STEP #5. PULL IT ALL TOGETHER

In the case of the Radisson Hotel DFW South, flow of funds and the lack of new construction were the dominant trends, but there were also the secondary influences of expected stronger job growth and overall improvement in the economy. We believed the hospitality sector is going to improve and would have targeted the hotel industry for additional investments over the coming three to six years. Investing ahead of the curve holds potential to offer great rewards. We will carefully monitor the market and activity of the trends closely in order to mitigate our interest rate risks.

Rely on Logic

There are many ways to invest in real estate. Most often we think about directly buying an investment property and then owning, operating, and eventually selling it. But recently, Hall Financial Group has expanded how we invest in real estate, in particular, in hotels. This process is called "structured finance."

Essentially, what we do in our structured finance business is invest in other successful real estate entrepreneurs. We are able to fill the financial gap between an asset's traditional mortgage and the available equity.

For example, let's assume you have identified a property you want to buy for $1 million. You have $200,000 of equity, but the only mortgage you can find is for 60%, or $600,000. The gap between the combination of that first mortgage plus your equity and the price is $200,000. What Hall Financial does is structure a way to provide the $200,000 until the property is able to support a higher first mortgage or in some other manner allow the property to repay our money, plus a material return. This concept of filling the gap is often referred to as "mezzanine" or "preferred equity" financing, depending on how the deal is structured. Returns on mezzanine or preferred equity financings often total 20% to 25%, when you factor in payments made along the way as well as the money received at the time we exit the investment.

The decision to make structured finance deals requires consideration of the same five-step process for identifying where your property is in a timing cycle. Much of what we learned about the Radisson Hotel DFW South was applicable to hotels in general in 2002. From our perspective, hotels were so compelling that we wanted to increase our investment in them. On the other hand, hotels are highly intensive to manage. Our goal was to find other entrepreneurs who had local market and management experience that could enable us to invest as a structured finance investor rather than a direct owner.

Let me take you through some of our thinking on why in 2002 and 2003 we became a very aggressive structured finance investor. In 2002 alone, we invested $40 million through structured finance and, as this book is being written, we are in the process of investing additional funds in hotel structured finance in 2003.

Our thought process starts with the lack of capital flowing into hotels. Particularly, the more conservative nature of first mortgages makes hotel financing difficult to obtain. This allows us to provide a very necessary and important service to hotel entrepreneurs.

For example, in Napa Valley on Highway 29, a group of entrepreneurs headed by Ned DeLorme and Sushil Patel had raised $1.8 million in equity and found a first mortgage of $2.25 million to construct a new hotel. They had a hole in their financial structure of $8.1 million. We negotiated a structured finance transaction that enabled them to go forward to build a Hilton Garden Inn. Without our money, it would not have been built. Instead of being long-term equity investors, which would have significantly diluted our partners' ownership, we agreed to a formula designed to provide us with a return of between 20% and 25%. Because the project was successful, they were able to pay us off in one year and, although we received a 25% return, they benefited by paying us off in a short time and getting their project built without equity dilution.

Another example is a group in Texas that was a minority partner in eight hotels. The larger partner wanted to be bought out in a short time frame and the minority partners wanted to have complete control of the project. We agreed to put up approximately $8 million, all of which was used to buy out the larger partner at a discount. We negotiated a formula that, based on how the hotels are doing, will provide a return of somewhere in the mid-20% range. In fact, the hotels have performed better than any of us expected and, so far, our returns just from immediate cash flow are in excess of 15%.

I could go on with other examples, but the point is that the lack of other sources of available funding has enabled us to provide a service to entrepreneur developers at a critical time. Because we are real estate people, not Wall Street MBAs, we understand and can work with entrepreneurs in a way that helps facilitate transactions. While not everyone can fill the role of providing structured finance, you should not be discouraged from creating a project because of mortgage or equity difficulties and should consider creative ways to fill the gap for funding a project to completion.

You should not be discouraged from creating a project because of mortgage or equity difficulties and should consider creative ways to fill the gap for funding.

And Then There's Hindsight

Yes, hindsight is indeed 20/20. And, if you stop and think about it, the thought that occurs just before "We could be in trouble" is "Everything couldn't be better." When you're in the middle of a market in which prices are getting ready to decline, that's when you're most likely hearing good news and excitement from investors confident about the future. The irony is that we often get caught up in the enthusiasm without stepping back to look at the facts available about current trends.

The thought that occurs just before "We could be in trouble" is "Everything couldn't be better."

It's only through thoughtful evaluation of the seven trends in combination with the anecdotal evidence that you really can identify your property's potential. It's hard not to invest at a time when everything seems to be exciting and positive. But if construction numbers are too large and job growth looks shaky, you've got a combination that equals potential trouble and must not be ignored. One way to make a lot of money in real estate is to avoid losing it. Minimizing your exposure on the downside is as important as maximizing your opportunity to make money on the way up.

One way to make a lot of money in real estate is to avoid losing it.

An interesting phenomenon is that many investors find it more difficult to buy at the bottom of a cycle than at the top. The whole psychology of buying when you know prices are low is a difficult concept. If low prices equal low values, then buying low can feel like you aren't very smart or that you aren't getting much for your money. This is especially true if you think prices will continue to fall—and all the more reason why I believe that careful evaluation of all the trends combined with consideration of anecdotal evidence is the best way to decide when to buy, how long to hold, and when to sell real estate.

When to Buy

Buying Basics

Most people are excited when they first buy real estate. They enjoy the thrill of the acquisition process and think about how much pleasure they will get from running the property—not to mention how much money they are going to make. The thrill is unfortunately and mistakenly tied to that second greatest lie I talked about earlier in the book: "Real estate is a cash flow business." Remember: the time to make money in real estate is at the time of sale.

Before you ever buy, you must think about selling. Buy with the mindset that the bulk of your profit will come when you sell. More to the point, you also need to consider when in the future you are going to sell and why your property will be worth more then than it is now. Most importantly, you should know what you are going to do to make your plan work. To eventually make a profit, you should create an investment plan and attempt to follow it. Inevitably, circumstances will change along the way and cause you to modify your plan. You won't ever know precisely when you will sell—it could be four, five, or even 10 years from the time you buy. But, barring unforeseen circumstances, you can and typically should plan to hold your investment for approximately five years. During this time, you should plan to improve the property, increase NOI, and ultimately enhance value.

As part of your planning process, be as specific as possible about the physical improvements you would like to make. Be thorough when projecting NOI (more information follows) and take a position on how you believe each of the seven major trends will affect not only your purchase decisions but also your anticipated holding period and your position at the time of sale.

Think Through Where Your Property Is in the Timing Cycle

To know where you are going, you need to know where you are. The information you gained by working through the processes in Chapter 6 should be used to establish your starting point. From there you can create your path to selling. It is critical to consider where you stand in the context of the typical lives of each of the seven trends and how each will position your property for future NOI and cap rate growth.

To know where you are going, you need to know where you are.

Determine Your Purchase Goals

We all have heard over and over that you're not going to get very far if you don't know where you're headed. This old saying holds true in buying real estate. Finding your investment goals are quite straightforward: you need to decide on the type of property you want, the general size range you can handle, the market location in which you're interested, and your intended purposes for the property.

Coming up with the type of property you want may be the easiest of these decisions. Let's say you are interested in rental homes. Maybe you are in a market area where single-family houses have appreciated and you think that owning and renting a second or a third home in a small subdivision can ultimately lead to profits. Indeed, that's one approach and a reasonable goal.

Investment size is often determined by your own financial ability. How much money do you have for a down payment? Investment properties usually require down payments of 20% to 25% of the total purchase price.

In terms of deciding on the area or areas where you want to concentrate your acquisitions, it's always best to go with what you know. If you have the opportunity to invest in locations in which you have experience but also happen to look promising, then that should be your priority.

The last but not least important of your goals is what you plan to do with the property. Do you want to invest in properties that can be improved substantially to gain more upside? Or, are you interested in properties that are in substantially great shape and require very little of your time and involvement? Both of these radically different approaches are fine, and your goal could also be somewhere in between. The idea here is to define your plan and your approach before you buy.

Finding Your Property: How to Effectively Use a Real Estate Broker

Professional real estate brokers can prove invaluable as you search for investment properties. Good brokers are well connected in the marketplace and can help you uncover multiple properties much quicker than if you try to do so on your own. Before making a selection, however, take the time to ask for referrals from associates in the field and meet with several prospects to determine personality style and fit for you.

Timing the Real Estate Market

Take the time to provide your broker with specific descriptions of your investment goals, with the understanding that the more you tell them the better job they can do for you. Walk them through the points we have already covered here so they will better know what types of properties to present to you.

You may want to work with more than one broker at a time if you are looking for multiple property types in multiple geographic locations. Some brokers and firms specialize in particular property types in specific market areas. And some brokerage firms have offices located around the world or at least are able to participate in national networks that can facilitate property searches based on the needs of individual clients.

The type of arrangement you enter into with your broker and their firm depends on all the variables associated with the purchase. Often the broker's compensation comes from sharing part of the commission paid by the seller to its listing broker. In some cases you will benefit by working exclusively with one real estate broker. If, for example, you are looking for single-family rental homes in a defined area, one may be able to scour the market and present you with all suitable opportunities. On the other hand, if you are looking for properties with a broader geographic definition that might involve a number of suitable options, letting several brokers know what your goals are might be a better way to go. As with all professional business relationships, be up front and forthcoming. Let your broker(s) know if you are seeing properties from multiple sources.

We are currently looking to purchase vineyard properties in Napa and Sonoma counties, and have selected two brokers who specialize in each of those counties. Both have presented properties to us and so far we have closed one transaction with each of them. Our best experiences have been with licensed professional brokers who have 10 to 20 years or more experience in the market. We rarely work with newcomers. Experience makes a big difference.

Even if you have entered into an exclusive relationship with one broker, you should always keep your eyes open for properties that may be for sale directly by owner. Reading newspaper advertisements, looking for "for sale by owner" signs on properties, and staying aware of what's going on in your market are all good ways to locate properties.

Get to Know Your Market: Getting the Word Out

You should talk to your business associates and network with as many people as you can about what you are trying to accomplish. In all cases, the more specific you can be, the better off you are. Start growing your contact list by collecting names, addresses, phone numbers, etc. Every time you meet someone, add him or her to your list and then—most importantly—stay in touch. You'll find that more deals will come your way if people know who you are and what you want.

Once you have purchased your first property, get the word out. If it's appropriate, issue a press release to local newspapers. If the transaction is large enough, send a release to the national trade media. Send a copy to everyone on your contact list. The point is to keep yourself in front of those people who can keep the flow of potential investment properties in front of you.

Appraisers, Market Studies, and Local Economic Indicators

Before you make a decision regarding your property, be sure to analyze area sale comparables that include information about other nearby properties that have been sold recently and are similar to the one that you have, if you already have one, or similar to ones that you want. Comparables help define the differences and similarities among the properties you're considering and help you evaluate current market conditions. You get this information from brokers, anecdotal discussions, and appraisal reports.

Usually lenders require appraisals, and your real estate broker may be able to direct you to appraisal information. Appraisers, in my view, provide mixed results. I don't rely on their numbers so much, because in essence they are hired to justify a specific price for a specific property. Still, the information in their reports can be very helpful and should include information about other recent sales of similar properties. Their reports often outline other economic indicators in the marketplace that could be valuable to you.

Appraisers, in my view, provide mixed results. I don't rely on their numbers so much.

Look for appraisers who have put in the time, effort, energy, and dedication to earn the "MAI" designation from the Appraisal Institute. This certification generally implies a greater level of competency, but don't just accept everything you are told. Appraisers often feel pressured to come up with the result that the client wants.

How to Find a Lender

Once you've identified a property to purchase, you need to start thinking about financing. If you are looking at single-family homes, a second home in a resort area, or other smaller properties, local lenders may be your best choice. Savings and loans can be good sources for this type of financing. Banks are generally good as well, but they often tend to offer shorter-term loans on investment property. If you have a fairly typical property in an area with banks and savings and loans nearby, make a simple phone call to see what they have to offer. A straightforward approach is always best.

In many situations, using a mortgage *broker* can be helpful. Mortgage brokers generally charge 1% of the loan amount to locate a quality funding source for you. Mortgage brokers can review multiple lenders who are interested in your project and, in the process, can often negotiate a better deal than you might have been able to get yourself. In these cases it is well worth the brokerage fee. We often use the services of mortgage brokers, but in some situations we also directly approach lenders with whom we've worked before.

A mortgage *banker* is yet another source of financing. Mortgage bankers differ from mortgage brokers in that they actually close the loan with their own funds and then later sell the loan to another longer-term lender. Mortgage bankers often pool and sell groups of loans rather than individual ones. This reselling of your loan should not impact you in any way and does not alter the rights or obligations of you as a purchaser or the rights and obligations of the lender. If you close the loan with a mortgage banker, it is the same as dealing with any direct lender. What happens to the loan following the closing does not affect you.

The Dangers of Leverage

Generally speaking, leveraging your investment can benefit you. Leveraging enables you to put down less of your own money when you buy a property. The higher your percentage of debt, the higher the return on your money. In other words, if you buy a property with 10% instead of 25% down, generally you'll make more on your investment, depending on interest rates. An added benefit is that with leverage you can often buy larger properties and "trade up" as you continue investing.

However, it is easy to get in trouble if you take on too much debt. Never depend on lenders or others to make sure you are not overextending yourself or to watch after your interests. Remember to regularly review the two greatest lies in real estate: "Capital improvement costs will only be $XX" and "Real estate is a cash flow business." In terms of how much financing you are able to carry, safety is your responsibility. And the higher your leverage, the more important this issue is to your real estate investing success.

Whether a property is heavily leveraged or not, always have a contingency plan in place. Make sure you maintain an adequate supply of cash reserves for unexpected capital expenditures and those inevitable surprises (e.g., new roof, new air conditioning system, etc.). Never count on cash flow for capital expense needs. It's fine to borrow as much as you can, so long as you understand the implications, including the risks of negative cash flow.

Remember to regularly review the two greatest lies in real estate: "Capital improvement costs will only be $XX" and "Real estate is a cash flow business."

Assuming Existing Financing—The Good, the Bad, and the Ugly

Many properties will have mortgages in place at the time they are purchased. Depending on the terms, you might be able to buy the property subject to that loan, meaning that the existing loan can become your loan. Many loans are assumable, but not all, and as the purchaser you would have to meet the lender's qualifying requirements and perhaps pay a transfer fee. (See the following for more information on recourse vs. non-recourse debt.)

Buying a property subject to its existing debt has several benefits. First, it's generally easier to qualify to become a replacement borrower than to qualify as a new borrower. Second, it takes a lot less time to qualify this way and it is simpler contractually, enabling the transaction to close sooner. Third, the existing loan may have a more favorable fixed rate than is currently available.

Buying a property subject to existing financing may have some great pluses, but it also may have some significant minuses. The loan may be at a lower leverage ratio than you could get with a new first mortgage. For instance, if the loan principal has been paid down some while the property has gone up in value, you may have to put up 30% or more as a down payment to pay the difference between the purchase price and the existing financing. At the same time, if you were to get new financing, you might be required to put only a 10% or 20% down payment toward the property. The interest rate and terms might also be less desirable than with a new loan, depending on market conditions. And, there may be other terms in the existing agreement that are unsatisfactory to you, such as the length of the loan, balloon payments, etc.

In many cases, if a property is already financed, you won't have a real choice about assumption. Many loan agreements don't allow for prepayment or the prepayment may be subject to such a high penalty that refinancing is just not practical. This means that if you really want the property, you must buy it with its existing loan, for better or worse. This can be ugly. We've already discussed some prepayment issues in earlier chapters and how they relate to interest rate timing trends. With commercial investment-grade properties, dealing with mortgages and prepayment penalties has become complex, limiting the flexibility and often the economic benefits for borrowers.

New First Mortgages

Financing most investment property is fairly easy to do. Your real estate broker should be able to refer you to good mortgage brokers. As just discussed, it is often well worth the 1% mortgage broker service fee to find out what the lowest interest rates and other terms are out in the marketplace—not to mention the amount of your time that will be saved. You should expect your mortgage broker to deliver three, four, or even more qualified options from reputable lenders.

As you work through the process of obtaining your loan, don't be afraid to ask that your broker negotiate specific issues that are proposed to you. Lenders do not negotiate readily and will often take the "Here is what I'm willing to do—take it or leave it!" approach. Yet, if you return with a small list of reasonable requests, you may find the lender willing to accommodate you.

New first mortgages can be fairly easy to get, though they take time. Your property purchase contract should be contingent on your ability to obtain suitable financing, so that if you can't get acceptable funding you won't lose money under the contract. Specifically, when you enter the "due diligence" phase of the deal—the process of verifying the financial and physical status of the property, based partially on information you have been given by the seller—you need to spell out contingency terms relating specifically to your ability to obtain financing. This is important, as the lender will want to be certain the property is worth what you're agreeing to pay—not for your benefit, but for the lender's own protection in the event of default.

Lenders do not negotiate readily and will often take the "Here is what I'm willing to do—take it or leave it!" approach.

If you're obtaining new financing, the seller needs to understand that after 60 or 90 days of applying for financing, if none has been secured as expected, you have a right to get your deposit or earnest money back and exit the purchase agreement. Make sure to include this provision that protects your earnest money if financing is not obtained.

Understanding Financing

No matter who your ultimate financing provider is, there are certain aspects of loans you should consider. Some of the most important include the following:

1. **Fixed Interest Rates vs. Floating Interest Rates.** You can borrow money with either a fixed interest rate or an interest rate that changes (or floats). Fixed interest rates tend to be higher than floating rates. The advantages are that the interest rate doesn't change over the term of the loan, so you have assurance of what's required for budgetary purposes. It is usually beneficial to

obtain fixed interest rates when you believe that rates are rising or seem quite attractive. Floating interest rates are best when you anticipate that rates will decline over time. These floating interest rates require you to be flexible with regard to interest payment expectations. Floating-rate loans generally have considerably lower rates than fixed-rate loans. These rates float, or change, over the loan's term every 30, 60, or 90 days, or whatever the agreement is between lender and borrower. Usually these floating-rate loans have low or no prepayment penalties, in contrast with fixed-rate loans, which can have substantial prepayment penalties.

2. **Amortization.** Amortization is the process of gradually paying down a loan's principal until it is paid in full. Typically in the loan's early years, more of each payment is allocated to pay off the interest than the principal. In later years, more principal and less interest are paid. Often loans do not fully amortize, but have a required earlier payoff. For example, you might have a fixed interest rate for 10 years, even though the property has a 25-year amortization schedule. Because the loan term is only 10 years, at the end of the term you would have paid off only a portion of the principal, with the balance being due as a "balloon payment." This is a common lending practice and, in many cases, the balloon payment is subsequently refinanced.

3. **Length of Loan.** The length of your loan can also vary considerably. Many are in the five- to 10-year time frame. When rates are low, we generally try to obtain financing for 10 years or longer. When we think rates are high and might be on the way down, we try to get five-year financing. The truth is none of us really know where interest rates are going and making these projections is not easy. Unfortunately, educated guesses about interest rate movement can be critical to your overall profits in real estate. Within your real estate portfolio, it is advisable to have a variety of loan lengths. One of the things I have learned from

years of trying to make interest rate predictions is that it's impossible to know with certainty what the future will bring. Hedge your bets whenever possible.

4. **Liability vs. Non-Recourse Loans.** Many real estate loans—particularly on larger investment properties—are structured so that you are not personally liable to repay the money. These loans are known as "non-recourse" loans. Essentially, you are borrowing the money, but only on behalf of the particular piece of real estate that is involved. The property becomes the sole collateral for the loan, and, other than accepting limited liability for unusual acts, such as stealing money or doing something contrary to the loan contract, you are not personally liable to pay back the loan and are really at risk only for the equity investment that you have already put into that particular investment. This is important and significant, because sometimes in real estate, when things go bad, they go very bad. You don't want to put yourself in a position where you lose your home and other assets because one investment turned out to be a disaster.

Many real estate loans ... are structured so that you are not personally liable to repay the money.

Commercial banks will almost always require your personal guarantee or personal liability before they make the loan. This is particularly true for construction loans and other short-term interim loans for a property purchase. In some states, should the property go into default, lenders will ultimately be forced to choose between suing you based on your personal liability guarantee and going after the property itself. Foreclosure laws differ from state to state and you should always be aware of what they are within each market area.

In all cases, you should thoughtfully consider whether you are willing to risk personal liability with the investment. Whenever possible, I think it is best for the borrower, and in many ways for the lender as well, to look to the property as sole collateral.

A great part of our real estate business today is making structured finance loans to other real estate entrepreneurs. We know what is involved from a lender's point of view and the loans we make are always non-recourse, with one exception: if the borrowers take cash flow from the property not specifically provided for in the mortgage agreement, the act of doing so triggers borrower personal liability.

Seller Financing

Sometimes owners will sell properties and finance them at the same time. This can be very simple, easy, and advantageous from a buyer's perspective. We recently bought a vineyard site in Sonoma County with the seller financing our purchase. We were able to negotiate a more flexible financing arrangement with a lower interest rate and more favorable terms than a bank would have done. As a result, we were willing and able to pay a higher price for the vineyard. In a sense, both parties won. From the seller's perspective, this is often an excellent approach to maximize value. From a buyer's perspective, particularly with unique properties like vineyards, seller financing can be an effective way to gain the type of leverage that ultimately will help produce better returns.

Seller financing can occur at two levels on a property. It can be the only loan on the property—essentially its first mortgage. That was the case with our Sonoma vineyard. On the other hand, a seller can make a loan that is separate and in addition to the first mortgage. This loan can help you get a lower down payment and higher leverage and can be a useful tool for the overall property acquisition structure. In such a scenario, the first lien holder on the first mortgage (such as a bank) will need to approve the seller's second mortgage. Often lenders will not approve a second mortgage as such, so you may have to structure the seller financing as a loan against your partnership or against the equity in whatever entity buys the property, assuming you create a separate entity to buy it. This is a sophisticated financing approach and is not necessarily right for all real estate purchases.

Mezzanine Financing

If a seller is unwilling or unable to provide seller financing, another form of leveraging the property, in addition to the first mortgage, is mezzanine financing. Mezzanine financing is a way to fund the difference or shortfall between the traditional first mortgage and your equity. A mezzanine loan is a middle-level loan, much like a second mortgage. It can also be a third mortgage or a loan against the property's equity without a mortgage attached to it at all.

These types of loans are structured finance tools that allow for increased opportunities for creative real estate investments. As mentioned previously, in response to market demand for this type of lending, our company formed a business unit that focuses specifically on mezzanine and structured finance lending for other real estate investors.

By their nature, structured finance transactions require a great degree of flexibility and creativity and are meant to help borrowers purchase a property, fund new construction, or implement a repositioning or renovation plan when other more traditional approaches won't work. If you can get the same money by obtaining a first mortgage, do so by all means. It will be a lot less expensive. Interest rates on structured finance transactions generally run in the high teens to the high 20%-plus interest rate range.

While you may think it strange that an investor would be interested, willing, and able to borrow money at a 25% rate, there are in fact times when it can be a great trade for both sides. At Hall Financial Group, we look for situations where our money, loaned over a three- or four-year period, can help make a project happen that would not otherwise have had the chance to happen. We look for situations where we can do well financially and also provide the borrower with the means to achieve his goal and also do well financially. In many cases, without our structured finance or mezzanine investment, there would simply be no project.

What Lenders Expect of Borrowers

Lenders have standard and routine expectations of borrowers, and as a borrower, you should plan to be held to these expectations. In my company, we expect at least the following:

1. **Truthfulness throughout the process.** Lending is based on trust. Like all lenders, we expect accurate, honest, and forthright information from every borrower. Despite this expectation, lenders should be realistic and know that borrowers may be enthusiastic, quite "sales-oriented," and perhaps a bit overly optimistic. At Hall Financial Group, if we think a borrower is intentionally being dishonest with us, that's all the reason we need not to do business with him or her. What we want is to work creatively and diligently to help make deals happen for borrowers deserving our trust.

2. **Borrowers must meet their obligations, both financially and otherwise.** Nonfinancial obligations include agreements regarding specific performance requirements, such as renovation obligations on a property. If borrowers do not meet their stated obligations, my company falls back on requirement number 1 above and expects a forthright approach to dealing with any problems that arise.

3. **To keep all of the cash flow from the property in the property or in the property's financing.** If there is an agreement in place that allows for cash flow distributions to the borrower, then that of course is fine. But if there is any level of default or deferment of debt payment, then we want the borrower to leave the cash flow that comes from the property in the property so that it is available for payment of the debt and the ongoing needs of the property.

Picking Your Lawyer

Retaining a good attorney to help get you through the buying process is important. One key to the selection process is choosing a specialist. You want to retain someone who spends all or at least most of his or her time practicing real estate law, not someone who is a generalist with little knowledge about real estate. Ours is a specialized field, and it's easy for lawyers to make mistakes if they are not involved in real estate contract work on a day-to-day basis.

You also want someone who is willing to work hard for you and who will take a personal interest in your work. Good lawyers are busy and, as with all professions, some are more conscientious than others. Don't underestimate personality either. It's important for you to like each other and get along well.

You also want someone who is willing to work hard for you and who will take a personal interest in your work. Good lawyers are busy and ... some are more conscientious than others.

Finally, I would recommend that you choose a lawyer who understands the scope of what you expect him or her to do. If you want help negotiating some of your deal's business points, then say so. But your lawyer should only be handling the specific items you have given him or her authority to handle—and only after specific discussion. Some lawyers will unfortunately get into the business side of the transaction without your authority to go there and can end up killing a deal before it ever has an opportunity to happen. Having a quality real estate lawyer is a true asset, but you need to control the process.

Reading the Sales Agreement

The sales agreement is a critical legal document that outlines all the details and considerations associated with your purchase. It covers all the obvious fine points of the purchase such as sales price, terms of payment, timing of closing, etc.

Buying Basics

The not-so-obvious details covered in the agreement are just as critical to your success as the obvious. Sales agreements typically document promises made by the seller about the property. These include fundamental facts, such as a statement of current ownership and the property's overall condition.

Representations made about the property condition are often controversial, as sellers want buyers to assume all the risk and vice versa. Statements about property condition as written in the sales agreement can be critical to your future success. Disclosures about condition are unique to each property, each agreement, and the warranty you receive from the seller. It is difficult for me to give you exact guidelines here other than to tell you to use your best and sound judgment, logic, and common sense. At times, negotiations about condition can become overly technical and can kill a deal, based on warranty demands that frankly aren't worth the worry. At the same time, you do need to think through the agreement's warranties to make sure you are covered in the event of major seller misrepresentations.

At times, negotiations about condition can become overly technical and can kill a deal, based on warranty demands that frankly aren't worth the worry.

Each sales agreement should outline the title you will be receiving for legal ownership of the property and spell out the due diligence period—a specific period of time during which you will conduct your own thorough inspection and study of the property. It is during this due diligence phase that you will have paid a deposit (the "earnest money deposit") toward the purchase that should be held by a third party—usually a title company—until the deal closes. This deposit, also commonly referred to as "good faith money," should be fully refundable up until a previously agreed-upon point in time (your "free look period"). All agreements associated with the handling of your deposit money should be clearly stated in the sales agreement.

If for any reason whatsoever, at your sole discretion, you should decide that the findings from your due diligence process are unsatisfactory, you should get your deposit money back in full. A good sales agreement is written to allow the buyer time to inspect the property prior to closing, with an option to be released from the purchase without penalty.

Title Companies, Escrows, and Closing

Earnest money, as provided for in the sales agreement, is generally held in a title company escrow account. Title companies provide the insurance that you will be getting the actual legal title to the property you want to purchase. When I first started out in business, title companies were used far less than they are today. Lawyers were relied on to locate and read the abstract or history of the property and then prepare a legal opinion of their findings prior to the sale. The problem with this was the rare instance when something would go wrong. It could be that the attorney who prepared the opinion was out of business or otherwise not to be found, leaving no recourse for what would turn out to be an unusual but nevertheless huge problem. That's why the use of title companies has become routine, with virtually everyone involved in a commercial real estate transaction obtaining title insurance.

In addition to providing needed insurance, title companies hold deposits and all other escrow money in trust accounts from day one of the transaction through closing. The title company also typically handles all details associated with the closing itself. Often buyers and sellers or their representatives will physically meet for the closing, but at other times transactions are closed by mail.

Regardless of how the sale is accomplished, on closing day the old lender gets a loan paid off, the new lender receives a mortgage on the property, the buyer gets the property, the seller gets a profit (hopefully), and any others with a financial interest get what they get. The title company is the neutral party that makes sure the deal happens as agreed in an honorable and trustworthy manner.

Due Diligence—A Critical Phase

During the time allowed for due diligence, you'll have much to accomplish. Make sure the sales agreement allows sufficient time for the process—typically 45 to 60 days—but at times as many as 90 days are needed. The level and intensity of review required depends a great deal on the size and type of the investment. Your lawyer can help you through this process also, but make sure you have time to do the following:

1. Check out all of the assumptions and representations spelled out in the sales agreement, including but not limited to the property's specific physical condition.

2. Verify property NOI. Remember that current NOI is where you begin in terms of cash flow projections, which has everything to do with your ability to survive until you sell. It's also your starting place for building a higher stream of NOI that will make your property more valuable when you sell.

3. Make sure you understand the market and specifically the property's primary competitors within the submarket. If you don't, then now is the time to study up on this information, researching what new competition could be coming to the submarket. Throughout this process, verify that the purchase of your property is at market price or lower. You can do this by reviewing recent recorded sales in the area (your broker should provide this) and comparing price per square foot or unit as well as capitalization rates. Also find out what your competitors are doing, including what is working and what isn't.

4. Validate your ownership plan based on what you find. Use this time period to learn as much as you can about your project's feasibility and to verify other specific aspects of your plan. For

example, if you're buying a piece of land with the idea that you would like to subdivide it into smaller parcels for resale, now is the time to get more data from the local governing authority responsible for approving subdivision plans.

5. Verify where you are in the timing cycles. The breathing room of the due diligence period will allow you to reconsider the whole idea of the purchase once again. More importantly, take a second look at where the property stands in the timing cycle. Ask yourself where it is likely to go during the time that you intend to own it. These are critical considerations and will determine whether or not you'll ultimately make money on this particular investment. Remember: at this point you still have the luxury to change your mind and walk away.

6. Review the expenses of the property carefully. This is where you can find either upside opportunities or pitfalls. Sometimes sellers are clever about hiding expenses in the year or two prior to selling. Check everything you can, including whether or not they were deferring maintenance. You might also find that operating expenses are too high, meaning you have a greater opportunity than you thought.

7. For most properties today, due diligence includes getting a third-party environmental report. When I started out in the business, no one ever thought about things like environmental studies, but today they have become routine. Phase I of an environmental study tells you whether or not the property is "all clear" or if it contains potential issues, such as an underground oil tank that needs to be checked for ground leaks. If the latter is the case, you will have to add a Phase II study. Costs for a Phase I study typically run $3,000 to $5,000. Phase II study costs vary widely, depending on what is involved to completely investigate and quantify the environmental problem. If you don't have these studies done and an environmental problem arises later, say a chemical runoff from a laundry facility that was there years

before, you may find you have some personal liability under a federal environmental statute. Federal laws can impose absolute liability for anyone who currently owns or has been in the chain of title to a property with an environmental problem, even if the owners were not aware of it when they owned the property. Also, environmental problems can stem from overflow of a contaminant from an adjacent property. If your property has environmental issues that warrant consideration, by all means, get the advice you need and reduce your risk for potential lawsuits in this specialized and complex area.

Federal laws can impose absolute liability for anyone who currently owns or has been in the chain of title to a property with an environmental problem, even if the owners were not aware of it.

---

8. Review the property's zoning and make sure it is in compliance. If there are any noncompliance issues, it is best to know now. Your local governing authority is the best source for this information.
9. Check out all the building codes that relate to your property and make certain it is in compliance. Most municipalities or local government authorities have some form of periodic inspection and corresponding certificate of compliance. Be sure to ask the seller for copies and check with the government authorities about any code enforcement issues of concern.

Renegotiating Your Deal After Due Diligence

After due diligence, many buyers routinely go back to the seller to try to negotiate a reduced price or different terms. This renegotiation or retrading process is becoming increasingly common. It is at this point that the buyer has nothing to lose and everything to gain—and the seller is strung out from waiting through the two- to three-month due diligence period for the sale to happen. He or she is motivated to complete the transaction and will often reduce the price and agree to modify the terms just to get it over with.

I believe this is bad business. That's not to say that there won't be occasions when retrading is entirely appropriate, based on discoveries from due diligence. Any renegotiation or retrading, however, must be reasonable, with detailing the rationale for needing to alter the original agreement. I retrade only when what we find is so far beyond a margin of acceptable difference that I would have no other choice but to walk away from the original transaction or adjust the price. In these instances, I often have ended up with a much different agreement overall than the one originally negotiated.

I believe this is bad business. ... Any renegotiation or retrading ... must be reasonable, with detailing the rationale for needing to alter the original agreement.

There is no doubt in my mind that if our company's buying strategy routinely included retrading we would have gotten somewhat better prices on many of the properties we purchased over the years. At the same time, I believe we would have gotten a negative reputation for retrading and, because of that, in certain situations where there has been buying competition, we wouldn't have been the chosen buyer.

Sellers can (and should) check out your reputation. What they find out generally about my company leads them to want to do business with us. We do what we say and, most importantly, we show up at the closing table. Sometimes there are delays and on occasion we have had to retrade. But in all cases we do not routinely retrade. Our approach is instead to try to positively verify all that the seller has represented in the sales agreement with a goal of closing the deal. In those rare circumstances where deal points had to be changed, we handled the situation in as direct and fair a way as possible—and then we closed the deal.

Structuring a Property Management Plan

If you are buying your second or third property of a similar type, then you probably already have a plan in mind for property management. If this is a first purchase, you may want to consider alternative ideas for how to manage the property on a day-to-day basis.

The first basic question is "Are you better off managing it yourself or hiring a third party?" The answer depends heavily on what type of property it is. If it were a small rooming house or a second home, then I would urge you to try to manage it yourself. Management can be difficult and aggravating but also highly rewarding. There is no substitute for knowing what's going on from hands-on experience. When I bought my first rooming house, I wouldn't have considered hiring someone else to manage it. Without direct involvement, I wouldn't have understood the results nearly as well.

Management can be difficult and aggravating but also highly rewarding. There is no substitute for knowing what's going on from hands-on experience.

There are other types of properties—such as hotels—that require more specialized property management before you jump in. While Hall Financial Group has owned and managed hotels over the years, our company never really had the ability to manage hotels as well as companies that specialize in it. For that reason, in 2002 when we bought the Wilson World Hotel and transformed it into a Radisson, we also looked for the best third-party management company we could find. We compared companies based on the quality of their operations, what they had done to help the hotels they manage make money, and how much they charged for their services. We hired the one we felt would do the best job and certainly a better job than we could and now we look to them for this expertise. We believe in this case we will benefit from someone else working hard for our needs and interests.

149

We also use third parties to manage our vineyard properties. In Napa Valley and Sonoma, we employ three companies. We are able to learn the best practices from each to help improve the quality of our grapes for the wine that we produce.

With third-party property management, make sure that you stay informed and aware, managing the big picture—your asset. The financial results, the physical condition, and the long-term plans for the property are broad asset management issues, rather than day-to-day property management issues.

With third-party property management, make sure that you stay informed and aware, managing the big picture—your asset.

Whether you decide to turn over management to another property manager or handle it all yourself, consider the pluses and minuses of each, establish a plan, and be prepared to take charge of your property one way or another the moment you close.

Timing and NOI Projections

As you create your plan to resell your property, realize that when you sell, prospective buyers are going to focus on the same things you were when you bought it—namely, NOI and cap rates. I've seen people over the years look at a property and think they'll be able to sell it for a bundle. Yet they never go through the exercise of projecting NOI out four, five, or six years in the future. Then there are others who use inflation rates as the only influence on NOI and assume that NOI will grow because of that alone. NOIs must be considered carefully when timing the eventual sale of the property. Cap rates in the future must also be considered, but they may be more difficult to project.

At a bare minimum, put pen to paper for each year of your holding period. What can you do that will make gross income go up? What can you do to lower expenses? What can you realistically expect to be spending each year? How much will it cost to make needed physical improvements? Are there marketing expenses and management modifications that can affect your overall income and cash flow?

No matter what you project, you'll certainly find that things turn out differently from your plan. Even so, the exercise of thinking through your plan gives you a critical baseline. Modify your plan regularly to keep it dynamic and think through the life of your property on its way toward your goal of making money.

Take It to the Board of Directors

This may sound odd, but for every property you buy, I recommend that you create a thorough written plan as though you were going to make a presentation to a board of directors or loan committee. Your plan should outline clearly what you are buying, why you are buying it, and what your plans are for the property. This document could be from five to 10 pages long and should include NOI projections as well as all the basics about the property's size, price, location, condition, etc.

Planning is more than important. I'm a big believer that in real estate there are more variables outside of our control than within it. You can do a great job running a property and still end up in foreclosure because timing was terrible. This certainly happened to many of us in the 1980s. However, despite the factors outside of our control, planning can substantially increase the likelihood that you will do well on your investment.

Buy When There's Blood in the Streets: The Contrarian Timing Strategy

"Buy when there's blood in the streets" means buy when others are selling out of fear or desperation. This is the epitome of the countercyclical or contrarian approach to real estate investing. It is my preferred approach and, although at times throughout my career I lost sight of my focus on timing, it remains the approach with which I am most comfortable. Basically, the idea is to buy before the real estate market begins to improve, when everything looks bleak.

How you apply this to your real estate investments, including the pros and cons of this approach, are discussed later in this chapter. First, let's begin with an example of one of my earliest attempts to "buy when there's blood in the streets." Because you are buying just when everyone else thinks it is the wrong time to buy, you most likely will feel like it is the wrong thing to do. Be confident in your belief that the market is ready to turn around. Alternatively, as the next story suggests, sometimes being young, naïve, and just going for it works too. The following story illustrates a classic bargain basement real estate purchase in the middle of a bleak investing climate, followed by a dramatic turnaround.

Because you are buying just when everyone else thinks it is the wrong time to buy, you most likely will feel like it is the wrong thing to do. Be confident in your belief that the market is ready to turn around.

Why Would Anyone Sell a 20-Year-Old a $1.6 Million Apartment Complex with Zero Down Payment?

I graduated a semester early from high school (though not because my grades were high!) and was already running the real estate business I had started. I was also driving 15 miles each way to take courses at a nearby college, Eastern Michigan University. I later switched to The University of Michigan, before dropping out altogether.

During my time at Eastern Michigan University, I became familiar with one of the worst student apartment markets the world has ever seen. The campus was self-contained except for a few apartment complexes that were a long walk or a short commuter bus ride away. Located on the other side of a beautiful river, these apartments suffered from a horrendous reputation in 1968 and 1969. They were not well occupied because of their distance from the campus and students thought they were "in the middle of nowhere." Things got even worse when a series of rapes and murders occurred there; parents couldn't imagine their children living on the "wrong side of the river."

With other student housing for competition, low overall demand, too many private apartments being built, and the unique problems of the murders and rapes, the Huron Hills Apartments were virtually a ghost town. At this point, I owned a number of older, small rooming houses and apartment properties in Ann Arbor. But to me the idea of buying something as huge as this 128-unit complex seemed both ridiculous and an impossible dream.

I've never been accused of thinking small, so it didn't surprise anyone too much when, after having watched Huron Hill's deteriorating condition for a while, I decided to go for it. I had watched the property decline further and further, and I knew it needed a huge effort to turn it around. Thinking about the challenges associated with this property caused me many a sleepless night, but I'd never been so excited about a project in my life as I was in 1970 when I decided to go for what I believed could be a great opportunity.

I've never been accused of thinking small, so it didn't surprise anyone too much when I decided to go for it. Thinking about the challenges associated with this property caused me many a sleepless night.

I was introduced to the senior representative of the owner of Huron Hills by my business law teacher at Eastern Michigan University, David Mackstaller. I still remember our first meeting as clearly as if it happened only a few hours ago.

After waiting in a gorgeous room, I was escorted into a huge executive office. To me, it looked like you could put a basketball court inside this office and the view was incredible. I was wearing my only suit and had cleaned up as best I could. But as a 20-year-old student landlord, I wasn't exactly what you would call the most professional-looking. Nevertheless, through David's connections and my aggressiveness and enthusiasm, there I was, meeting with one of the owners of Huron Hills.

"So you're interested in buying Huron Hills?" the owner asked.

"Yes," I replied.

"How much down payment do you have?" he asked.

"None," I answered.

Now, in most situations, that would have been the end of the conversation. I later learned that these were desperate people entering desperate times.

"No down payment could be a bit of a problem," he said. "But let's see if we can come up with a creative solution."

From the time of that meeting in late May of 1970 until August 1, when we closed on the property, I was living in a dream. Totally unknown to me, affiliates of the selling group had been loaning themselves money through a bank that they controlled. Between having a first and second mortgage on the property securing the loans they had made and having lost a lot of money on the property, they were in default on their loans and desperate to sell. Without a doubt, this situation contained all the ingredients for a unique opportunity—motivated sellers with conflicts of interest, banking regulators breathing down their necks, a need to get their names off the mortgages, and a terrible local market.

No one with any brains at all would have bought into the "wrong side of the tracks" real estate market, yet, there I was. Young, optimistic, and not knowing any better, I did it with partners. David became my partner, along with an older, more sophisticated real estate broker named Duncan Robertson, who added a sense of dignity to our group. The total purchase price was $1,641,000—and my only investment as of the closing date was the money I spent on parking fees and gas to get in and out of downtown.

No one with any brains at all would have bought into the "wrong side of the tracks" real estate market, yet, there I was. Young, optimistic, and not knowing any better.

We had our work cut out for us. Of the 128 apartment units, only 20 were occupied. Yes, that's right: we had just purchased 108 empty apartments. Moreover, our apartments all came "furnished," but it was mostly trashed. As part of our transaction, Bank of the Commonwealth agreed to loan us money with a third mortgage that we used to buy new furniture.

Nobody could have worked any harder than we did to turn Huron Hills around. We changed its name to Eastern Highlands and began an aggressive marketing campaign that involved a little character we created as the official mascot of the property. He soon rivaled the mascot of the University. We named him after my brother Scott, created "Scotty Sayings," and printed them on stickers that were soon found on automobile bumpers, in dorm rooms, and all over town. Some of the Scotty Sayings were risqué and quickly became one of the cool things around campus. We started a shuttle bus service so that students didn't have to walk back and forth to school. The bus also took our residents to local bars and restaurants. This was particularly appreciated as there was still serious concern about crime. But fears began to fade with increased security and as we cleaned up and filled the property with tenants. Once the property gained acceptance, we opened "Scotty's Club" in a restored basement on the property where the residents could gather to socialize. We threw frequent parties, usually on Sunday afternoons, with free beer, pizza, and movies.

Before long, every one of the 128 apartments was occupied. Not only had we turned Huron Hills around, it had become the "in" place to live. Our "buy when there's blood in the streets" strategy had worked.

Huron Hills was not the only property we bought when no one else would. In fact, doing so became our company trademark.

What Is Contrarian Timing?

Contrarian timing is trying to buy at the bottom of a cycle when a market is at its absolute worst. It's buying when others are selling, when people are afraid, and when many people have already lost a lot of money.

If buying at the bottom and selling at the top is a good idea, why doesn't everybody do it? Because it isn't easy to do. The normal emotions that control our entire decision-making process clearly move us away from buying at the bottom. Even beyond these emotions, it's not until after the fact that we know for sure when the market hit bottom.

Contrarian timing is buying when others are selling, when people are afraid, and when many people have already lost a lot of money.

When trying to use contrarian timing, you must be careful of falling knives. There's an adage in investing circles: "Never catch a falling knife." It's dangerous to grab a knife before it hits the ground or a declining investment before it stops going down. In other words, if you think you are buying at the bottom but are actually buying on the way down, you can end up suffering significantly or even losing everything. More than one bottom-fisher has gone broke in this process. It's not as simple as it may appear.

When trying to use contrarian timing, you must be careful of falling knives. It's dangerous to grab a knife before it hits the ground or a declining investment before it stops going down.

Do Markets Always Rebound?

Early on I was sure every market was certain to rebound and that it was only a matter of time. Most markets do, but sometimes more slowly than you would like. But, in general, real estate markets are cyclical and what goes down *will* come up again.

But guess what? There are exceptions. Staying in touch with the local trends unique to each market is key. If a market decline is demand-driven, the market could have a long-term problem. Reasons for a rebound should be clear from the beginning. A national economic recession is one thing, but a change in local market trends that could be permanent—like out-migration—is quite another. It's important to closely evaluate the trend shifts.

Local market oversupply is usually something more cyclical than out-migration. If demand is traditionally strong for single-family homes, office space, or other types of real estate, but supply outstrips demand for a certain period, you'll usually see a slowdown or a halt in new construction. Time typically will cure this problem. How much time depends on the rate of absorption of the existing over-supply. Absorption is the difference between new demand for the real estate product and new available supply. For example, if 100,000 square feet of new office space is built and 300,000 square feet of office space is leased, the result is a net absorption of 200,000 square feet of existing space for that particular market area.

You must learn to consider causes of the bottom of the market as you see them, reasons why the market will soon take a turn for the better, and about how long that should take. Don't bet the store on your predictions, because it's impossible to be precise. The best you can do is get the trend right and the timing close.

Five Principles to Live by When Making Contrarian Investments

1. **Have a Plan.** If you're going to be a contrarian buyer, it's more important than ever to plan your exit. Put together a cash flow analysis. Consider where you are in the cycle, what you need to see a turn around, and how long that process will take.
2. **Think About What Can Go Wrong.** When you plan, always think about what could go wrong. Outline your expectations. Then do it again from an even more conservative perspective.
3. **Make Sure You Have Extra Cash.** Look at your most conservative plan and make sure you have the cash required to weather that storm—or at least know how you could get it if you need it. Staying power is everything.
4. **Be Positive and Provide Leadership.** When making contrarian investments, deal with people from a confident and positive position. Provide honest and sincere leadership. Let others know what

your plan is, where you are now, and where you're going. Admit along the way when you make mistakes that cause you to veer off track.

5. **Don't Believe Your Own Press.** Going against the norm, you're more likely than others to become well known. When things go well, don't believe it will last. When things go badly, don't believe that either. The truth of the matter is, if things are going well, more likely than not it is because of good timing, as opposed to your pure brilliance and skill. Likewise, if things are going poorly, it's likely not all your fault. Either way, the point is to keep moving forward and remember that you're accountable only to you—not the world. Do the best you can do—and don't accept defeat.

Risks and Problems with the Contrarian Investment Approach

1. **It's a Lonely Strategy.** One of the problems with being a contrarian is emotional. Rationally, it sounds easy to buy at the bottom, hold, and then sell at the top. It sounds so logical that people even joke about it and suggest that it's just doing the obvious. Yet, in practice, it's anything but easy.

   Emotions cause investors to feel that at the bottom things are perhaps at their riskiest time. After all, the bottom is full of negative information about why things haven't been going well. For instance, in the mid 1980s, overbuilding caused office buildings to plummet in price. It was hard to see how or why things would ever get better. Words like "never" and "ever" are often used and are often wrong. At the bottom, generally, there is a prevailing pessimism that's easy to accept. It's a lot easier to go with the flow than to be a maverick.

2. **Financing Will Be Tough.** Financing a contrarian investment is much more difficult than a mainstream investment. Banks, savings and loans, insurance companies, and most lenders don't understand

or agree with the idea of buying contrary to market trends. If they are willing to finance you at all, it will be on an ultraconservative basis. For a contrarian, seller financing is often the solution, because financing through third-party lenders is very difficult.

Part of what makes a contrarian play work, however, is the overall restrictiveness of lenders. Your opportunities can be greater, because everyone else sees only risks and the competing supply of new properties will be limited. In a way it was helpful that lenders stopped making hotel loans in 2000-2002 when we began to buy because it limited new supply.

Your opportunities can be greater, because everyone else sees only risks.

---

3. **Markets Don't Always Turn Around.** You have heard the saying, "Everything cycles." Well, the fact is that everything doesn't cycle. As discussed earlier, in Flint, Michigan, it seemed like a good idea to buy homes really cheap, but the market simply never came back. Moreover, even if things do cycle, but it takes a very long period of time for the cycle to turn upward, it's still a poor investment. The fact is, you need to look at the seven trends and the vibrancy of any particular market area and then make sure that you're buying a property type in an area that at least shows promise for an up cycle.

4. **You Can Be Too Early and Lose Even if You're Right.** Buying contrarian, I have made the mistake of buying too early, which can be extremely expensive. If you're buying a property that's losing money, but you think in time it will stop losing money and have a positive cash flow, that all sounds good. But what if your timing is off? You can be right with your plan, but if you lose money for an extra two or three years, as I have done in the past, the project can be very painful.

One of the keys to contrarian investing is to have enough reserves and staying power, both financially and emotionally, to stay the course and ride things out when they don't go exactly as expected. Remember: things often don't go as you project. The reality of owning real estate is that it rarely performs as you or others would expect it to on paper.

One of the keys to contrarian investing is to have enough reserves and staying power, both financially and emotionally, to stay the course.

Bottom-Line Benefits

While the risks and problems associated with contrarian investing should be serious considerations, I still favor this approach for two basic reasons:

Relative Safety. It may sound odd, but most people feel safer buying property (or, for that matter, stocks) at high prices. I look at the comparison to the replacement cost, the historical marketplace, the seven trends and their impact on the considered investment, and my general anecdotal knowledge of any marketplace. Based on all of that information, I always would rather buy when something is temporarily out of favor. I say "temporarily" because I have learned through hard lessons like the one in Flint, Michigan, that not everything cycles up again. However, most things do. While most people seem to be happy paying high prices and hoping they stay high, I believe it's safer to pay low prices and wait for them to rise.

Biggest Rewards. When you are right with a contrarian investment, you are very right. You can reap huge rewards quickly by buying at or near the relative bottom of a market cycle.

Buy When Prices Are Going Up: The Momentum Timing Strategy

"**B**uy when prices are going up" means buy once it is clear that the real estate market is starting to recover from a low point in the cycle. It is basically a momentum investment strategy. You let the cycle's upward momentum carry the price of your property higher, in combination with any improvements you make, and then sell before the market cycles back down again.

The momentum investment strategy can be applied to any real estate class. Because you are buying after it becomes clear that the markets are turning around, you need to be able to act quickly to purchase your investment, but also be prepared to sell quickly before the markets turn back down again.

Later in this chapter, I will explain in more detail how you can use the momentum investment strategy in your real estate investments and will discuss the pros and cons of this approach.

But first, you may recall from Chapter 6 that raw land is the asset class most strongly affected by the path of progress trend. Further, raw land can be an exceptional property type to purchase using the momentum approach. The story that follows outlines how my company used this strategy to purchase several large parcels of land in the far northern area of Dallas just when real estate markets there were about to recover.

Raw land can be an exceptional property type to purchase using the momentum approach.

A "Path of Progress" Momentum Play

It was 1989 when Hall Financial Group put together a fund to invest in raw land. We were looking for opportunities that would capitalize on the momentum of the upward cycle. We planned to purchase and hold these investment properties as prices rose to even higher levels. In analyzing different areas in which to invest, we relied on some of the basic trends.

We looked closely at the path of progress trend and saw that, in general, growth in the Dallas area was moving consistently far to the north. The successful northern suburb of Plano had been the recent location of choice for multiple property types, but now the path was moving beyond Plano. The area we identified as a potential future hot spot was Frisco.

We then looked at Frisco's in-migration statistics and saw that the city was growing rapidly. We also investigated the area's new construction and found an inadequate supply of new construction to serve the city's growing population.

We also looked at new construction trends in surrounding communities and found that land zoned and available for new apartments in particular was in short supply. So with the new construction trend working in our favor to limit the supply of competing properties, we began to focus on land in Frisco that was already zoned for apartments. We also reasoned that public opinion in many communities could be turning against more apartment development, making it highly likely that future additional zoning for this property type would become even more restrictive.

With these multiple trends working in our favor, we were convinced that investing in and around Frisco was the thing to do. We looked at several strategic path-of-progress locations and identified one site we believed was going to be right in the heart of substantial new development. It was literally on Dallas's main north-south transportation artery that leads directly into Frisco, the Dallas North Tollway. Moreover, this site was just across the tollway from an area that was planned to be a large regional mall. We were enthusiastic about the potential we saw and ultimately purchased a total of seven parcels in Frisco.

All of our Frisco area investments in the late 1980s and early 1990s turned out to be good ones, based in large part on our careful analyses of the local trends and our general plan to buy with the upward momentum. During this same period, national economic trends were moving up and down. At times they were even all against us—especially in 1992. As we always buy with a predetermined plan to sell, we originally thought we would sell these land purchases fairly quickly. But as it turned out we were forced to hold many of the sites far longer than projected. We eventually sold six of the seven parcels quite profitably. And, we had been considering selling the last site to an apartment developer before we decided to make a significant commitment to develop the land ourselves.

This last 162-acre tract is now known as Hall Office Park. It is an award-winning multi-tenant office community that lies at the crossroads of two major thoroughfares. It is in close proximity to what has turned out to be the largest regional mall in North Texas, a brand-new multi-use sports complex, a minor league baseball stadium, and a variety of other residential, retail, and entertainment venues.

Momentum buying can be a safe and profitable way to invest in all kinds of real estate. The key is to do your homework and carefully consider each of the seven trends. In the case of our Frisco acquisitions, history has proven we were right.

Momentum buying can be a safe and profitable way to invest in all kinds of real estate. The key is to do your homework and carefully consider each of the seven trends.

What Is Momentum Buying?

Momentum buying is simply the purchase of real estate when an upward trend is clearly established. You will be able to recognize times when the trend is clearly going down, times when it is clearly going up, and times when you just can't be sure. To make successful momentum purchases, you've got to be sure the cycle is on its way up.

But how can you know for sure? When prices have stopped falling, have begun to stabilize, and are beginning to move up—that's your first signal. And the sooner you recognize it, the better off you will be.

Five Important Indicators of Upward Momentum

1. **Positive Direction of the General Economy.** If the general economy is in a recession, headed in that direction, or potentially at the top of an upward trend, then it's not a time to catch upward momentum. If, however, the economy is improving, coming out of a recession, or continuing an upward trend, then momentum is moving in your favor.

2. **Positive Job Growth.** On both a national basis and within any given local market area, positive job growth is a key indicator of positive momentum.

3. **Positive Money Flows.** If money is flowing into real estate, whether from foreign sources, a change in investor direction, or general

increases in money supply, the point is the same: increased flow of funds is an indicator of positive momentum.

4. **Stable or Falling Interest Rates.** Stable or falling interest rates are positive momentum trend indicators on a broad basis.

5. **A Positive Prevailing Psychology in the Marketplace.** When people are generally positive about real estate as a favorable investment and prices seem to be going up, it's a good time to catch positive momentum. Watch for prices to start rising on the type of real estate you are looking to buy.

Buy to Sell

The key to successful momentum buying is when to get out. You must sell in order to capitalize on the trend. With each and every investment, never forget to plan how you are ultimately going to realize your profit. When you buy, have a sale date in mind.

As I will discuss in more detail in Chapter 12, holding onto your property for one full upward cycle (buying low and selling high) is the general idea. But if you are a momentum buyer, it is more critical than ever not to hold a property too long.

How Momentum Buying Is Different from Contrarian Buying

Contrarian buying, as detailed in Chapter 9, can be risky business—much more so than momentum buying. As a contrarian buyer, you are using the seven trends and anecdotal information to recognize when a downtrend seems to have been extended. It is at this precise moment that you need to pay some attention to figuring out just where the actual bottom might be, as you are going to try to buy before the upward trend has been clearly identified. Herein lies part of what introduces the risk to contrarian buying.

Momentum buying, however, is buying as soon as possible after you recognize that an up cycle has clearly been reestablished.

Four Risks and Problems with Momentum Timing

1. **Missing a Lot of the Move.** If you're a true momentum buyer, you're watching the market cycles carefully and waiting until you see an upward cycle clearly in process. You almost always will miss the first part of the move and, depending on the duration of the cycle, you may also miss a great deal of the cycle's upward momentum. If, for example, you buy one year into an upward cycle and ultimately the upward part of the cycle lasts two years, you would have missed half of the upside.

2. **Short Cycles.** A short cycle may not be appropriate for momentum buying, because short upward cycles can last as little as 18 months or less. Short cycles can make the momentum strategy particularly difficult and challenging.

3. **Long Cycles.** Long cycles can also be confusing. Sometimes upward trends last for an exaggerated period, making you believe you're making a momentum buy when you're actually buying into a market anomaly. During the mid 1980s, for example, property prices continued to rise even as economics were deteriorating. Investors justified higher prices by pointing to rising inflation and the added support of tax benefits. While both reasons were valid, the basic laws of nature and simple cash flow economics also needed to be considered. In other words, the "false" momentum was undercut by several underlying downward trends that ultimately burned a lot of investors.

4. **Possibility of Staying Too Long.** Holding too long can turn a momentum strategy into a disaster if the market for your property collapses. What made things even worse for momentum buyers in the mid 1980s was that it was hard to know when to sell. In the middle of that historic era, it seemed that prices would rise forever. Then, in 1986, the tax laws were changed retroactively, the economy deteriorated, and prices began to free-fall. It was impossible for everyone who wanted out to get out.

How to Spot the End of Upward Momentum

As explained at the start of Chapter 7, each real estate cycle has four parts: an up cycle, a plateau, a down cycle, and the bottom. And each cycle is different. The upward portion of a cycle can vary in length from two years or less to four or five years. This part of the cycle will also vary in degree of movement, meaning some cycles will move only a few ticks at a time and others will skyrocket.

For these reasons, predicting the duration of an upward cycle and whether or not you've seen the plateau is not easy to do. After all, if a bell rang at the top and bottom of each market cycle, we would all theoretically be trying to jump in and out at the same time.

The good news is that there are ways you can learn to ring your own bell by looking at the seven trends and the anecdotal market evidence. This analysis requires that you stay in touch with the local trends, consider the impact of the national trends, and listen to what you hear in the marketplace. It is neither important nor likely that you will consistently pinpoint the top of a momentum move. What is important is that you generally get it right and sell while momentum is still moving up. You are better off getting out too early, leaving some money on the table, than waiting too long and running the risk of missing your sales opportunity altogether.

From experience, I know that waiting too long is an easy mistake to make. It's easy to avoid selling when everything is still looking up. You can get complacent and stop thinking about where you are in the timing cycle. But if you're going to succeed with your plan and maximize profits, you need to constantly be thinking through the timing of the cycle and planning to sell. More often than not, you'll surprise yourself at how close to right you can be and how taking the courageous step of selling when you are afraid it might be too early will ultimately benefit you.

Bottom-Line Benefits of Momentum Buying

When you've properly analyzed the direction of the cycle and know you're buying with an early upward trend, momentum buying is generally a much safer approach than contrarian buying. Those of us who prefer to make contrarian investment moves sometimes find ourselves catching falling knives when we buy before the market hits bottom. Contrarian buying can be exciting and extremely profitable, but the risks are greater. If your overall goal is to have balanced, safe returns, momentum buying offers better risk/reward opportunities with strong internal rates of return over shorter periods of time.

Part
Four

How to Hold

Increase the Value of Your Property: Six Powerful Techniques

With good timing decisions, you can maximize your returns using either the contrarian or the momentum strategy discussed in the prior two chapters. Hopefully, you can also maximize the benefits of the effects of the real estate cycles on property pricing.

You cannot, however, maximize total overall returns on your real estate investments with timing alone. During the time you own an investment, you should take advantage of every opportunity to increase its value—and ultimately its sales price—through steps that are within your power.

Principal ways to increase value during your holding period include improving the physical condition of the property, improving operating and expense efficiency, and improving the marketing of the property. Specific ways in which to improve your property are discussed later in this chapter. Generally speaking, try to time improvements so that the market will pay for them. In other words, if a market has high vacancy, you may not want to spend dollars on improvements or marketing that won't increase occupancy.

Try to time improvements so that the market will pay for them.

The stories that follow show some practical examples of how my company improved the value of one of our large apartment communities and how we intend to improve the value of a new vineyard property we recently purchased.

"Holding" a Property Often Means "Get to Work"

When we first looked at buying the Rigi Vineyards in Napa Valley in 1996, all of the property's 500 acres were for sale but at a price we did not think represented a good opportunity for us. The owners thereafter sold about half the land to another buyer and continued to market the remainder.

In 2002, we decided to make an offer on the remaining 230 acres. The price per acre had been substantially reduced from what we had considered paying six years earlier. During our due diligence work, several problems came to light that, under normal circumstances, would have caused us to walk away from the purchase altogether. But we ultimately believed this acquisition was in my company's long-term best interest and chose to negotiate further with the owners. They agreed to lower the price further, but required a large amount of cash at closing. As it turned out, we ended up paying one of the lowest prices per acre for Napa Valley vineyard land in recent history.

The property was riddled with problems, but in our view none that couldn't be overcome. Vineyard land, just like single-family homes, apartments, hotels, office buildings, or other improved real estate, can become a deferred maintenance nightmare. Immediately apparent to us was the property's poor accessibility. Its only entrance was poorly located and accessible only by way of dilapidated bridges spanning several streams. Reconditioning the bridges and roads alone would cost about $1.5 million, but doing so will greatly enhance the property's value.

Another problem was the prior owners' failure to maximize cash flow. The Rigi Vineyard was planted solely with Chardonnay grapes. The pricing of Chardonnay wines had substantially dropped, so grape sales were down and cash flow was suffering, but the owners had made no effort to diversify to build cash flow. In prior years, the Rigi owners maximized cash flow by simply deferring maintenance. Improvements such as replanting and road and bridge repairs, all of which we believed should have been done, had gone undone.

The former owners' efforts to salvage the vineyards through "savings" resulted in a unique opportunity for us. During our holding period, we plan to take advantage of the opportunity to rebuild, replant and diversify product, and generally improve the land.

As we do this, we also will take advantage of what I call "bonus opportunities." The Rigi property happens to consist of three separate parcels. We found that, under California law, we could divide the land into six legal parcels. Resale prices for smaller single parcels of land cumulatively can be higher than for larger tracts, so one option we see for maximized value is to divide the three parcels for resale.

You should always explore multiple uses for any given property.

We also are taking a fresh look at an asset that had been used in only one way for many years. Even though this land is known as vineyard property, we see its potential for different uses. We are in the vineyard and winery business, but we see ways to enhance the economics of the property, including selling the smaller parcels to individuals for single-family homes. In doing this, we would retain all the benefits of owning the grapes surrounding these homes, as well as the benefits of having sold land to people wanting to build single-family residences. We aren't sure yet whether we'll pursue this idea or not, but this is the type of creative thinking that can increase the value of an acquisition substantially. You should always explore multiple uses for any given property, even if you don't intend to follow through on all of them.

Turning a Big Lemon into Lemonade

One of the best examples in our company history of increasing the value of a property during a holding period is a property we bought in Michigan in the 1970s called Knob on the Lakes. I decided to buy Knob on the Lakes fully aware of its troubled history. Many folks thought we were buying a lemon, so—as a tongue-in-cheek jab at them—we renamed it Lemontree.

On January 1, 1975, my family and I were headed to San Juan to get some sun. As you may have surmised by now, business is never far from my mind. So, as we were driving to the airport, I saw a large property called Knob on the Lakes that was well known in real estate circles for its serious financial problems. I decided on the spot that this was going to be our next acquisition.

I didn't consider it to be much of an issue that—with 1,145 apartment units, a golf course, and a lake—this one property was equal in size to the rest of our entire apartment portfolio at the time. I've never lacked ambition and have always looked at problems as opportunities. Believe me, there were plenty of problems for us to turn into opportunities here!

I've never lacked ambition and have always looked at problems as opportunities.

Problems Were Not in Short Supply

High on the list of problems we inherited were the financial problems. The property had been planned to be 1,600 units over time and the existing 1,145 units had been built in phases over four years. The market could not absorb this number of units and the rent projections had been wildly optimistic. Therefore, virtually every financial obligation was in default. There were $2 million in delinquent mortgage payments, $1.2 million in unpaid construction costs, and $200,000 in utility bills outstanding—with the electricity company threatening to cut off the power at any moment. Oh, and the property was operating at a negative cash flow of about $170,000 per month, getting it ever deeper into the red every day.

You're probably wondering why I was interested in buying this property. Many of my friends and employees were asking the same question. First, I am an entrepreneur to the core, I like challenges, and this was a challenge like none I had ever seen. Second, I believed that my company could turn the situation around. Ultimately, we did just that.

First, let me tell you the rest of the problems. Then I'll explain how we created value out of this financial disaster.

PROBLEMS

First, the property was located 30 miles away from Detroit in what was referred to as "exurbia"—far from the center of the city. Although today living in a suburb far from your work is common, it was not the case in 1975. This negative was compounded by the fact that this was the era of gas shortages and rapidly rising fuel costs. The idea, even if appealing, of living in a far-off suburban area was dismissed by most as cost-prohibitive. Second, the property was beginning to fall into significant disrepair because there was no money for maintenance. Third, the property was less than 60% occupied and some of the residents should not have been allowed to rent. The owners had become so desperate to fill up the property that they had been renting to people who could not meet their monthly rent obligations. Finally, the rental market in the area as a whole was overbuilt and generally weak.

The first thing that I had to do was reach a deal with the seller and with the creditors. Because the emphasis here is on improving the property value, I simply will say that the negotiations were intense, very lengthy, and extremely difficult. The seller had his life savings and his personal pride tied up in this property and it was hard for him to accept the reality that he was about to lose it. The lenders and other creditors, like the seller, found it hard to believe that I, being 25 years old at the time, actually could pull all of this together.

OUTCOME

It took almost two months just to reach an agreement with the seller, which was contingent upon working out deals with the creditors. This took many more months. However, after we completed the purchase, all the changes that we made began a slow process of building our credibility and everyone's faith that there eventually would be light at the end of the tunnel.

We ended up purchasing the property for $25 million with no down payment. The seller received the hope of getting some of his money back out of the property. After we had put most of the preliminary financial agreements in place, we had limited partners enter the deal. Through our partners, we raised $3.3 million, which we used to cover the continuing negative cash flow for the first few years and provide capital for upgrades.

In 1985, roughly 10 years later, we sold the property for $42 million and the seller got everything we promised him. Additionally, all of the lenders and creditors received what was negotiated and our limited partners were paid large cash returns even in excess of their investments, while receiving a great deal of tax benefits along the way.

Building on Positives

If there were only problems, even I would not have been willing to entangle my company in the Lemontree mess. Instead, there were quite a few positives about the property that I thought could benefit us.

Although Lemontree had begun to show some signs of neglect, we found it to be extremely well built. The grounds and amenities were impressive and included a golf course, a swimming pool, tennis courts, and a clubhouse. The landscaping was top-notch. The lake was pretty, stocked with fish, and large enough for boating and other water sports. The individual apartments were well appointed; many included amenities that were at the time rather uncommon, including fireplaces and washers and dryers. Finally, the location overall felt secluded, more like a resort than a typical apartment community. With these exceptional amenities, and with a team of my highly motivated turnaround experts who were willing to roll up their sleeves and work night and day, we began to make a solid plan.

Every Transaction Needs a Management Action Plan

I first introduced my concept of Management Action Plans, or MAPs, as I call them, when writing *The Real Estate Turnaround* in 1978. The six techniques for improving the value of your property as next described will help you create your own MAP—a plan for how you will add value to your property.

> Don't ever buy properties that are already in perfect condition. Always buy opportunities.

The key principle is, don't ever buy properties that are already in perfect condition. Always buy opportunities. Ask yourself what about the property you are going to improve to enhance NOI and how that will in turn improve the bottom-line profit when you sell. A creative imagination and a willingness to think outside the box are important. Opportunities are plentiful, but too often we're held back by focusing on what can't be done instead of what can be done. Think positively and investigate every potential upside you can imagine.

There are six major areas of opportunity in a Management Action Plan:

1. Make cosmetic improvements and catch up on deferred maintenance.
2. Undertake major rehabilitation.
3. Improve the economic uses of the property.
4. Improve operational efficiencies, including cutting expenses without deferring important maintenance.
5. Improve the marketing of the property to prospects to increase gross income.
6. Reengineer the financing on the property to maximize returns.

Your MAP Needs an Alternative Bonus Plan

Even if you have your Management Action Plan in place when you buy, you should have even more ideas or plans that you can't fully count on at that time but that, if implemented, could significantly increase the property's value. I call these "bonus opportunities."

With our Rigi Vineyard, the bonus opportunity has to do with the option of subdividing and selling smaller parcels and retaining the rights in the plants on the property. This idea is still unproven and in need of research; we may or may not decide to move forward with this opportunity.

Think creatively and broadly when you buy. Think big. Think differently.

The point is to think creatively and broadly when you buy. Think big. Think differently. If you know you can make good money with your basic Management Action Plan, anything else you do above and beyond that is even better.

MAP Opportunity #1: Make Cosmetic Improvements and Catch Up on Deferred Maintenance

The best money you can spend on a property is often for minor cosmetic improvements. In most cases, the improvements with the highest payback are simply paint and carpet. In addition to these, add new furniture and fixtures. These types of customary improvements can make a big difference.

In other circumstances, because necessary maintenance was deferred too long, your first focus shouldn't be cosmetic improvements. Deferred maintenance issues come in varying degrees, all the way up to major rehabilitation. The larger the problem, the bigger the construction project to fix it and the more risk you face. In worst-case scenarios, deferred maintenance issues can include structural problems.

Unless you receive big purchase price discounts, for which you should negotiate before your money is committed, structural issues can be a serious drawback. They're not only expensive and difficult to estimate, but also invisible. Even though potential tenants or buyers can't see them, they still demand attention, but without the higher paybacks of cosmetic and other similar repairs.

Despite the risks and complications associated with repair or rehabilitation as a result of a previous owner's deferred maintenance, there are also corresponding opportunities. It is important to be careful in doing your homework and pricing the cost of your rehab plan before closing. Through the due diligence phase, if you learn that the property is much different from what it was represented to be, either don't go through with the purchase or talk to the seller about what you found. Sometimes sellers use the due diligence process to learn exactly the same things you need to learn about improvements and will often adjust the pricing accordingly.

As mentioned earlier, many of the physical problems with Lemontree were relatively minor and cosmetic. However, the upkeep in general was poor and perceptions among the residents and potential residents were not being addressed. We put a great deal of emphasis into making sure that the property was kept clean, that available units were spotless and ready to be rented, that maintenance requests were responded to promptly and completely, and that the landscaping and grounds were maintained at the highest levels. We responded to each and every comment or question received from our residents and analyzed what action needed to be taken to resolve their concerns. It was only after a few months of our attention that attitudes changed and residents began to compliment us on the good job of property management we were doing.

MAP Opportunity #2: Undertake Major Rehabilitation

When you're facing major rehabilitation, count on cost overruns and time delays because of the scope of the work required and the reality that you must be prepared for things to go awry in the rehabilitation process. The larger the rehabilitation, the greater the risk. At the same time, major renovations can present major opportunities.

Just a few years ago—partly out of a love for the city and partly because of a business I had in Europe—my brother-in-law and I began to look at the hotel market in Paris. We first thought we were just making a contrarian play with real estate there, but later found that Paris hotels had legitimate economic opportunity. I also believed that the value of the American dollar was high compared with the French franc, providing a bonus opportunity.

We eventually purchased one old, two-star hotel in an A+ Paris location. There were no four-star hotels anywhere nearby—interesting, given the location, practically in the shadow of the Eiffel Tower. Even though it was now my hotel, I wouldn't have recommended the place to anyone I know, nor would I have felt comfortable continuing to operate it at all in its poor condition. As a result, we began to plan major property renovations.

While building a brand-new hotel would have been less expensive in this situation, obtaining the right or entitlement to build one in that location would have been impossible, given the complicated and lengthy approval processes in Paris. This created a major barrier to entry for new competition. Redeveloping the existing hotel was the only way we could end up having the best of both worlds. Through the purchase, we obtained the entitlement to have a hotel of the same size as the existing hotel. We also had the benefit of the historic architecture that Paris loves. After rehabilitating, we would also have modern wiring, plumbing, and other conveniences hotel guests appreciate. It was a major rehab project, but because it was unique it offered great possibilities. We gutted the entire building and rebuilt everything from scratch.

The hotel just recently reopened, featuring guestrooms with modern amenities and unique appointments, such as original artwork over the headboards of each bed. Around the world exist similar locations and opportunities for major redevelopment projects that can be successful because of their uniqueness, barriers to entry, and exclusivity.

We likewise rehabilitated the Lemontree apartments, but on a smaller scale. The only significant capital improvement we made was to renovate the clubhouse. We repainted, changed the carpet, and added new furniture and accessories. Even this was not costly in terms of what most capital improvements can run. But, like the smaller upgrades, it made a big impression on the residents. Everything we improved served to further convince them that we were for real and seriously interested in their being happy living at Lemontree.

MAP Opportunity #3: Improve the Economic Uses of the Property

Before buying, think about what additional economic uses the property could have. Years ago we purchased an apartment community with an oversized recreation facility and an indoor tennis club. These "amenities" were ridiculously huge and ended up being burdens to the property's NOI. At the time of purchase, the seller disclosed all of the expenses associated with operating these facilities and we paid a lower price for the property than we would have if it had simply included a more typical clubhouse, pool, and tennis court.

Before buying, think about what additional economic uses the property could have.

After we modernized and improved the tennis and pool facilities, we offered the amenities in the form of a private club, with residents of the property receiving complimentary memberships. Our tenants appreciated both the physical improvements and the enhanced services we offered, and the new membership fees charged to those outside the apartment community helped defray the renovation expenses. After our third year of operation, these facilities were profitable and had proven to be a substantial bonus.

Our plans for the Rigi Vineyards are similar. Assuming that we proceed as planned, we will subdivide the property and sell off land parcels while retaining the rights to the grapes. And we will continue to look for ways we can economically benefit the property. While most see vineyards as land exclusively for growing grapes, we see much more. We see not only farming grapes, but also great home sites and potentially even greater additional winery sites.

Health clubs and tennis facilities within apartment communities and home sites within vineyard properties are only a couple of the many ways you can add economic uses to a property. With expanded profit centers and improved NOI, you can greatly enhance the value of your property and improve pricing at the time of sale.

MAP Opportunity #4: Improve Operational Efficiency

It's generally a lot easier to increase gross revenue than it is to cut expenses. But both are important and should be considered. No matter what type of property you own, in addition to expanding its economic uses, you can improve operations and NOI in other ways.

NOI is one of the two critical components that determine property prices. Any method you can come up with to cut expenses and improve operations directly falls to the bottom line. While new sources of income are great, they often come with additional expenses. But every dollar saved directly benefits NOI.

With every property acquisition, take a hard look at taxes early on. Is your property over-assessed? If so, don't be afraid to hire consultants or lawyers to make inquiries and appeal valuation decisions.

Next, consider insurance and any and all other controllable expenses. Every property has a narrow band of controllable expenses, but they all must be carefully reviewed. Remember that some seemingly obvious ways to reduce costs should be left alone because it would mean cutting quality as well. Still, if things can be done more efficiently, by all means, get moving in that direction.

Additionally, carefully review staffing costs. At Lemontree, for instance, although the majority of our focus was on increasing revenues, we evaluated the existing staff when we purchased the property. We then cut some staff members who we felt were not performing to our standards and we eliminated positions that were unnecessary. We also lowered other expenses, such as property taxes and insurance. Further, we were able to realize the economies of scale benefits (reduced supply costs and maintenance fees) associated with grouping the purchasing and service needs of all our properties.

MAP Opportunity #5: Improve Marketing

All the changes we made at Lemontree helped us reposition the property's identity so that we could generate higher revenues. From a revenue-generating standpoint, the vast majority of our focus at Lemontree had to be on bringing in new residents. The only way to do this was to get people in the door to see how great the property was.

Never underestimate the power of marketing. Increases in revenue can never be directly attributed dollar for dollar to marketing costs, but on an incremental basis, marketing has great value. For rental property, anything and everything you can do to improve occupancy, lower vacancy, or increase rental rates is a big benefit.

Never underestimate the power of marketing. Increases in revenue can never be directly attributed dollar for dollar to marketing costs, but ... marketing has great value.

Every piece of real estate has a reputation. The name of the property and its associated reputation carry brand value.

Some reputations are difficult to overcome. The Rigi name, for example, had become synonymous with lower-quality grape care; even though the grapes were produced in a good location with hard-working managers, the shortcuts being taken were known. As a result, the grapes produced there consistently received low bids from wineries.

One of the marketing initiatives we are taking at Rigi now includes renaming and rebranding the area as Napa River Ranch. Within the vineyard property itself, we are renaming parcels of land into individual vineyard areas as they are redeveloped. Each vineyard will be carefully marketed to complement the winery buyers' grapes and to service their needs. We'll coordinate this with the precise timing of harvesting the grapes. It's our intention to go the extra mile to do everything we can to please the needs of the wineries. It may sound strange, but the reputation and detail involved in marketing grapes is critical. More important yet is that good customer service must back up the perception created by positive marketing. This is true in every business.

Good customer service must back up the perception created by positive marketing. This is true in every business.

Keep in mind that improving marketing does not have to be expensive. As you'll recall, at Huron Hills we created a mascot for the apartments, made bumper stickers, and had pizza parties on Sundays. All of these efforts required only minimal costs, but resulted in fully leasing a property that was virtually empty when we bought it.

Similarly, Lemontree had developed a poor reputation among its residents and had almost no recognition outside the property. This was a big problem because we had hundreds of apartments to fill. We also needed to replace some of our current tenants: some weren't paying rent and some simply weren't desirable for the property.

The marketing plan we developed for Lemontree was one of the most elaborate and effective in the history of our company. Some of the key elements we employed should be considered when you buy rental property:

1. **Turn the residents into an extended sales staff.** From the moment we took over the property, the fullest attention possible was placed on making the existing residents happy. All the steps I mentioned earlier about maintenance, cleanliness, and attention to detail improved the feeling the residents had about the property. After we changed their perspective, and only then, we sought their endorsement. Among other promotions, we offered a $25 reward (worth more in the 1970s than today) for every new resident referral. This became a popular and effective tool.

2. **Keep the residents focused on the positives.** It took us a while to make the big changes needed at the property. In the beginning, we held resident parties and delivered a monthly newsletter to let everyone know about all the things that were being improved,

big or small. One of the most significant things we did to make residents happy was to increase security. Before doing this, we personally interviewed as many residents as possible and sent surveys to the rest. They told us they were concerned that security was not adequate. We immediately increased our number of security patrols. Each time we responded to residents' issues, we told them about what we had done in the newsletter or at resident gatherings.

3. **Make sure the whole market knows that the property is new and different.** We planned and implemented an elaborate grand opening celebration to rename the property Lemontree. We didn't change the name until we had made major improvements in the physical property and in the perception among residents. The grand opening was planned in secret and even the residents didn't know about it. Then, in a 60-day blitz of media, we announced the new name and new ownership. Over the first weekend of our grand opening, more than 3,000 people turned out to visit the property. Even with our lofty expectations, this was a huge number.

4. **Sell the sizzle, not the steak.** This is an old saying meaning sell people on the experience. We focused the marketing campaign on selling potential residents on the fact that they could in effect "live at a resort." This was during a time when gas prices were sky-high and people were unwilling to drive large distances from home to work. Many of them, however, would take weekend trips and drive much further than our property to get to a place with a golf course, pool, tennis court, clubhouse, and lake. We decided to market with a "Why not live at the resort all week?" concept. Once prospective residents saw how beautiful the property was, they were hooked.

5. **Make your property unique and memorable.** In conjunction with the name change, we based our identity on the "lemon" angle. Our maintenance staff became "lemon-aids," our leasing agents

became "lemon lassies" or "lemon laddies," the clubhouse was decorated and painted in yellow and green, the entire staff wore yellow and green coordinated outfits. One of our marketing slogans became "Apartment Living—With a Twist." In short order, it would have been difficult to find someone who lived in the Detroit area who didn't know about Lemontree.

6. **Have the residents help maintain high standards.** Over time, the residents became so pleased with Lemontree that they adopted our philosophy as their own. Most would let us know if another resident was not keeping the area around his or her apartment clean and many would do special things to improve the areas around their own buildings and apartments. There were frequent gardening contests to see which tenants could make their areas the most beautiful. You cannot place a monetary value on this level of commitment from your residents.

MAP Opportunity #6: Financial Engineering

Always look to see how you can improve your property by continuously reviewing its financing. Stay on top of interest rate changes and consider the possibility of refinancing at lower rates for higher amounts of money with greater future flexibility. Real estate financing has become extraordinarily complex, and lender requirements can make or break cash flow. It's important to consider your financing options on a regular and routine basis as part of your Management Action Plan.

There are no crystal balls when it comes to knowing the ups and downs of interest rates. The key, however, is to know the importance of financing your real estate. Even if you purchase a property without the best financing, constantly look for ways you can improve it when opportunities come your way.

In the case of Lemontree, financial engineering meant keeping the property alive long enough to give us a chance to turn it around. After months of negotiations with lenders and creditors, we arrived upon a framework. Most of them really didn't believe we had any chance of actually succeeding, but we eventually did.

Financial engineering should—and even must—be tackled anytime. Depending on opportunity, flexibility, and market conditions, you should always be ready, willing, and able to refinance.

Timing Your Improvement Plans

It's important to time your expenditures for when they'll do the most good. Operating cost cutbacks are always good and should be considered during downturns and upturns. Marketing expenses and improvements can be best tolerated during more robust markets—although they're often needed most during tough times.

Time your expenditures for when they'll do the most good.

Physical improvements are best made near the end of a downturn. If you're in a cycle that's turning up, consider major physical improvements so that, as the market gets stronger, your property will be better positioned. On the other hand, if you spend a great deal of money to reposition and improve a property in a market that's on its way down, you may suffer from high vacancies without achieving your goals.

Hold Most Properties for One Up Cycle

Holding properties during a real estate cycle downturn can be painful. During all real estate downturns, rents decline while expenses tend to stay the same or even increase. As I mentioned in Chapter 2, cash flow can go quickly from positive to negative. Therefore, generally speaking, your goal should be to hold your assets for only one up cycle and sell near the top. There are exceptions that we will review in the next chapter. However, the approach I favor is to use the seven trends to purchase properties at or near the bottom of a real estate cycle and sell at or near the top.

The story below relates one of my company's well-timed purchases, where we bought at the low point in the cycle and sold at the high point. Because we completed both the purchase and the sale within one cycle, we did not have to experience a new down cycle.

Selling Your Fruit Tree at Peak Harvest Time

1981 to 1982 was a down period in the real estate markets. We took advantage of this opportunity to aggressively buy properties at depressed prices. Emboldened by our success in buying during the prior downturn, we purchased 33 properties in just two years.

In 1981 we bought a 256-unit property in Pontiac, Michigan, a far northern suburb of Detroit. As was customary for us at the time, we gave it a "tree" name, like virtually all of the other properties in our portfolio. The tree had come to represent our company and was part of our logo. We considered the tree to stand for strength, dependability, and shelter. This new property was renamed Cherrytree Apartments.

It turned out that the downturn was relatively short-lived, as we had hoped, and Cherrytree's operations began to improve as the rental market picked up a year or so after our purchase. We put significant money into capital improvements to the buildings and the rental units, with special emphasis on the property's general appearance, which had badly faded. We painted the entire property and put in extensive landscaping. This helped with the overall image, especially when combined with our more responsive and customer-friendly management team and our emphasis on treating the property like a community. We held frequent resident mixers to allow everyone to get to know each other and our management team.

Sometimes, when you put yourself in the position for good things to happen, fortune decides to shine upon you. Shortly after our purchase, a new 800-acre industrial park was built near Cherrytree. This brought many new jobs to the area and people eager to live close to where they worked.

Occupancy at the time we purchased Cherrytree was in the mid-70% range. It was at 97% when we sold the property. Not only was the occupancy much higher, but also the tenant profile was much better as well, as we had weeded out the undesirable tenants. Some were required to leave when we failed to renew their leases, but most left on their own due to significant rental increases. Our improvements to the property allowed us to increase rental rates substantially over the five years we owned it.

We had paid only $5 million for Cherrytree in 1981 and we sold it at the end of 1986 for approximately $6.8 million. Combined with the tax savings that were inherent in all of our limited partnerships, our limited partners had an extremely favorable return on their investment.

The sale of this property in 1986 was an example of perfect timing in the cycle. As discussed earlier, in 1987, the real estate markets began a deep downturn that did not end for many years. The only disappointment I have about selling Cherrytree is that we didn't sell many more of our other properties at the same time. We were selling Cherrytree on its local market timing cycle and were not paying adequate attention to the national real estate timing trends. Had we done so, we could have seen that trouble was on the horizon.

So, How Long Is a Cycle Again?

Typical real estate cycles vary in duration from two to 10 years; within those various cycles, prices range from top to bottom. The seven major trends described in Chapter 5 interact to pressure the cycle up and down.

Each cycle will be different for each individual property type in each local market area. For example, it's possible that in Los Angeles apartments may be in a cycle that lasts six years during a time period in which retail shopping centers are in a cycle that only last four years. The impact of the national trends influences both apartments and retail, but the local trends might cause one cycle to be longer than the other.

The unique interaction of the seven trends affects different property types in different locations and causes the length of each cycle to vary considerably. There is no simple way to predict the exact bottom or top. There are, however, many signs or clues you can take from changes in the trends that often occur before real estate cycles change, because real estate cycles lag somewhat behind the trends that drive them.

Part of what moves the trends is human nature. For example, when things are going well in an upward cycle, it's human nature to build more new supply than is needed for any given type of real estate property. Our business system is based on competition and real estate investors and developers are always trying to meet and exceed the needs of any given property market. While the supply side is volatile and affected by human nature, the demand side is somewhat counterbalancing.

Part of the counterbalancing is that no trend can keep going in one direction forever. Indeed, even in a hot market, there always will come a time for at least a pause in the local trends, if not a time when there is less job growth, less in-migration, maybe even changes in the path of progress. An oversupply of real estate eventually will drive the prices of real estate down. A decrease in anticipated demand for real estate, whether from a lack of new job creation or a lack of in-migration, eventually also will drive the prices of real estate down.

National trends are also leading indicators. For example, knowing the direction of interest rates tells you one important element of influence. Real estate cycles will lag behind these trends, so seeing and understanding the trends in advance can be quite useful.

Why You Hold for One Up Cycle

In most cases, one upward cycle provides a sufficient amount of time to implement and complete your property Management Action Plan and reap its rewards. Selling when a property is relatively fresh with a new coat of paint and new carpeting helps you capitalize on both its top physical appearance and its overall perception of quality.

On the other hand, waiting for the next up cycle can create a backlog of capital improvement needs. You may be forced to defer physical improvements and maintenance. If you hold too long, over time you often spend too much money in capital improvements, defer maintenance too long, or a combination of both. These situations will hurt your investment.

The Impact of Deferred Maintenance on Your Plan

Back to the greatest lie in real estate: *It only takes $XX to cover needed real estate improvements on this property.* Anticipated capital replacement reserves are almost always less than what you'll really need.

Most new buyers upgrade their properties shortly after they buy. That upgrade is usually geared for the life of one cycle. Upgrades rarely will withstand two full real estate cycles. For example, new carpet, exterior paint, and other improvements likely will not last two cycles, which could easily run 10 years or more. Property upgrades create a selling opportunity—but if you wait more than one cycle, they become a selling liability, because the paint has lost its shine or the carpet has become worn out, meaning that either you or the prospective buyer have to upgrade again.

Hotels are perhaps the ultimate example of a real estate product type that, after two or three cycles, can go from a good-looking rehabilitated property to a property in a downward spiral. If a hotel has had insufficient maintenance and few capital improvements, daily room rates are hurt. A lower rate means lower income and even less capital to make future improvements. It quickly turns into a vicious cycle. A combination of normal "replacement reserves" plus front-end capital contributions from a new purchaser is usually the best way to maintain a property's condition. In this scenario, a perfect holding period is from four to seven years.

As described in Chapter 8's discussion of due diligence, when you buy a property, usually you should contract for an engineering report. I take these reports with a grain of salt. In most cases, financial burdens from deferred maintenance will be higher than the engineer's report indicates.

If you were to keep a 10-year capital expense log, you might find to your surprise that the expenditures remain at a consistently high level throughout. Even after your initial improvements, there are ongoing chronic maintenance issues that come up unexpectedly. Roofs wear out, water heaters go bad, cement sidewalks crack, asphalt driveways break up, and on and on. It's a reality of any older property. The older the property, the more chronic the deferred maintenance issues will be.

How well a property was originally built also matters tremendously. In the Midwest, where properties in general were built better than in the Southwest, we used to have less deferred maintenance. Our theory was that because of the cold weather, properties were better insulated and more attention was given to making them structurally sound. But even the best of buildings have maintenance problems that when repaired can't outlast one full real estate cycle. All of this ultimately leads to the conclusion that holding for one cycle allows the next owner to bear the burden of the next round of maintenance and consequently benefits you.

Financing Affects Holding Time

The best time to sell a property is when it can be financed at favorable rates. If interest rates are low, your buyer can maximize leverage at the time of purchase and can afford to pay you a high price. On the other hand, if the buyer can't finance the property in an economically viable way, he or she is forced to put more capital into the property and most likely will be subject to a less than favorable interest rate, forcing down the selling price.

Many real estate loans are structured as five-, seven-, or 10-year balloon loans. This means that the mortgage is amortized over a 25- or 30-year period, but must be paid off early, i.e. in the fifth, seventh, or 10th year with a large balloon payment. The good news with this type of mortgage is that the prepayment penalties are low, or even sometimes nonexistent, during the last six months or year. As the loan gets closer to maturity, penalties for prepayment are usually reduced lower and lower.

Beginning the selling process when a loan is one or two years from maturity is ideal. This provides the seller with more flexibility in timing the sale. It also leaves the buyer time to review refinancing options prior to purchase. If you market your property for sale too close to the end of the loan period, both the buyer and you may be pressed for time to complete the sale before the loan matures.

One Cycle Allows Time for Property Improvements

Since my old days in the rooming house business, I always made detailed physical improvement plans. My general idea was to do something to the property to make it better. Buying real estate with the idea that it will increase in value just because you now own it makes no sense. If you want to do this, invest in real estate investment trusts (REITS) in the stock market.

> Buying real estate with the idea that it will increase in value just because you now own it makes no sense. If you want to do this, invest in real estate investment trusts.

But if you want to be an outright direct investor in real estate, you'll usually need most of one entire up cycle to make a difference. Successfully implementing solid improvement plans can take three, four or five years. But once those plans are executed, it's likely that you're at the top of your value structure. Without an improvement plan, your property still may increase in value, but it will be at a much slower pace.

Why You Sometimes Hold for Less than a Full Up Cycle

When we talk about holding for a full up cycle, we're generally looking at holding for the majority of that cycle. For example, if a cycle is six years, you may be looking at generally holding for four or more years. But there are exceptions. There are unusual times when you might only hold for less than two years. In those cases, the reasoning to hold for less than a full cycle has more to do with the timing aspects of the specific property in the context of its operations and events rather than just the timing of the real estate cycle itself. There are two major reasons to hold for less than a cycle: if you see a real downside coming or if you've achieved your major goals.

IF YOU SEE A REAL DOWNSIDE COMING

This is one of the most difficult things to see. But if you are constantly analyzing the market, you should look for signals about the future and use those as a reason to sell at any point.

If you are constantly analyzing the market, you should look for signals about the future and use those as a reason to sell at any point.

For example, in 1984 and 1985, the market for apartments throughout most of the United States was increasing rapidly. We were waiting for another two or three years to reach the top. But if we had been watching the cycles closely, we would have known to sell. The new construction trend alone was signaling to sell. There were so many more units being built in most markets than could possibly be rented. In retrospect, it was obvious. Hindsight is, of course, clearest, but any thoughtful review of new construction could have shown in 1984 and certainly in 1985 that we were headed for a dramatically overbuilt market.

Even if we weren't sensitive enough to the dramatic sell signal from the new construction trend in 1984 and 1985, by 1986 the new tax law change should have opened our eyes. True, in some ways it was too late and prices were already starting to come down, but nevertheless we should have been listening and sold everything we could as quickly as we could. We didn't sell because we were blinded by our focus on growth. The dominant natures of the flow of funds trend in 1986 and the new construction trend throughout the early 1980s were such strong sell signals that anyone following the principles of this book would have sold their apartment properties by 1986.

Similarly, overbuilding in the office market in the 1980s was also a big clue to sell. Again, new construction was the dominant trend. Another trend that should have been obvious in many markets was that of slowing job growth. Finally, again, the flow of funds was slowing because of the tax law change.

These are examples of times when it is right to consider selling no matter when you made your purchase in the cycle. I say "considering" because each situation is unique. If you have enough reserves and feel you want to ride out the downturn, then you are making a conscious timing decision to hold. My biggest concern is not whether you act on every sell signal, but whether you think through the downsides that you are facing and consciously decide to hold.

Quite frankly, we didn't know all of this in the 1980s and didn't make a conscious decision. Ultimately, it ended up causing huge financial losses for us. With our greater focus today on timing the markets, the same thing is less likely to happen to us again.

If You've Achieved Your Major Goals

If your property improvement plan is substantially complete in an unusually short time, then you should be mindful of the reality that you've probably already increased the value of the property to at least close to its near-term potential. At this point, your future price increases might be limited. In many cases, it's good to lock in the value you've created by selling quickly.

Leasing empty space is one way that you can achieve a major goal and increase value. Dramatically raising the rent on a space that comes up for renewal is another example. Finishing and renting an addition to a property would be yet another example. In addition to these three circumstances, there are many others, but the key is that generally your NOI dramatically increased by repositioning your property and that selling may be the appropriate option even if the cycle remains favorable.

As you'll read in the story of the Judiciary Center below, we achieved a major goal quickly in a down cycle and sold that property for a huge profit. It can happen and, when it does, don't be afraid to take your profit and get out fast.

JUDICIARY CENTER: A SHORT HOLD THAT NETTED MAXIMUM VALUE

In 1986, the Washington, D.C. office market was dismal and, being the contrarians we are, we were considering buying a property. General Electric Credit Corporation, the lender to the prior owner, had foreclosed on an 11-story office building in a prime location that had been developed in June 1983 on a speculative basis, with no guaranteed tenants.

On the positive side, from our perspective, was that new construction in Washington was way down and job formation looked to be on an upward swing. In-migration figures also were good, because Washington grows from government opportunities bringing new people to the city on a regular basis. Our timing as contrarians could have been way off when we agreed to purchase this building, but fortunately it was not.

Hold Most Properties for One Up Cycle

The building was empty, however. We were trying to find a tenant to lease the entire building. But if we didn't, dividing it into a multi-tenant property was feasible. Though trying to find a single tenant can be feast or famine, the purchase price was low enough that we were prepared to hold on until we found that single tenant.

We got lucky. The biggest and best tenant you can get in Washington, D.C. is a government tenant. We leased the entire building to the U.S. Department of Justice and renamed it Judiciary Center. Even though we had plenty of interior construction to complete to satisfy the Justice Department's requirements, we were extremely enthusiastic. We had a 10-year net lease with the best tenant one could find, the U.S. government, on a solid real estate asset with a bright future.

Only mere months later, Japanese investors became interested in Judiciary Center. Their money flow was high, for the reasons discussed earlier. These buyers were looking for what they perceived to be relatively safe but trophy investments. And they were willing to pay hefty prices. After all, they were borrowing money in Japan at rates that were extraordinarily low compared with the standards of the day, bringing it to the United States, and buying assets at what for them would be a much higher return.

You've got to be willing and able to sell when the time is right.

We sold Judiciary Center for a 150% profit to Japanese investors in April 1987, just 11 months after we bought it. Our investment holding period was short because our plans for the property were completed much more quickly than we had anticipated. If we had held the property much longer, we may have made more money but we also could have made less. You've got to be willing and able to sell when the time is right. The timing was right for Judiciary Center.

When You Miss the Window, Waiting Out Another Cycle Can Cost a Lot

Prices vary by as much as 60% between trough and peak. Likewise, on the way back down, delays in selling can be costly. Waiting beyond the peak in any given market can mean a longer wait than you expect. Cycles are not uniform; when you think you might hold on just a little longer, instead of selling, prices may turn and begin to move down, so you're suddenly past the peak.

If you see this downward turn and think you'll benefit by holding and waiting for the next upward turn, you could be talking about five to seven years. And a lot can happen in those five to seven years. Operations may decline, local market trends may shift dramatically, and you may find yourself in big trouble with a property you can't sell and can't afford to hold.

Remember the second greatest lie in real estate: *Real estate is a cash flow business*. In a downward cycle, your cash flow early on can be impaired. By the middle of the cycle, cash flow could be gone altogether. And by the end of the cycle, you could be deep into negative cash flow and writing checks just to avoid foreclosure.

Therefore, it is better to sell a little too soon and lose some potential upside than to miss the opportunity to sell for what could be a very long time. That is why holding for just one up cycle is optimal.

Hold Some Properties Longer Than One Cycle

There are exceptions to the rule of holding for only one cycle. As discussed in the last chapter, if you miss your timing window and property prices fall, you can be forced to hold for the next up cycle. One positive reason to hold your property longer than one cycle is if it possesses unique attributes that outweigh the goal to sell. Following are two examples of unique properties we have owned and had discussions about why I elected to hold them for a longer term.

Willowtree, the Cash Cow

In 1981 we were buying apartments and raising money through limited partnerships. While I'd like to take credit for knowing in advance that Willowtree was a clear exception to the "hold for one cycle rule," the truth is that we discovered the project's extraordinary ability to produce positive cash flow along the way.

Willowtree is a two-property apartment community in Ann Arbor, Michigan, with a total of 475 units. Originally known as Village Green, it is located in the University of Michigan's North Campus area and at the time catered primarily to graduate students and young professionals. Even in 1981, this part of the campus was fairly built up.

We were motivated to buy Willowtree. It was during the time of our purchase that the U.S. government created certain incentives to encourage investment in real estate. As already mentioned, depreciation schedules were cut to 15 years and were also being accelerated. With these shortened depreciation schedules, the bulk of the related tax benefits could now be realized within the first five years of owning a property. And since the typical real estate cycle spans five to seven years, these government programs made the theory of holding a property for just one cycle seem even more reasonable.

But, some 22 years later, we still own Willowtree. The reason is simple: we have no idea how to begin to replace the magic of this property. It is a cash machine. Even after investing money each and every year to keep it in top-notch shape, we have a significant positive cash flow. We've refinanced it three times—and each time we have taken a substantial portion of our investment back out and provided cash distributions to our limited partners. Our investors have been paid back in full and, as the general partner, so have we. Still we continue to earn meaningful returns from cash flow alone.

I have often asked myself what makes Willowtree's cash flow so substantial, unique, and dependable. The answer I keep coming up with is twofold: we've got a good physical product and it's in a great location.

The quality of the property is a function of the excellent design of both the individual units and its exterior and how well it was originally built. Even though it is now 35 years old, Willowtree looks modern and new.

Its location is exceptional. The property sits inside an area with in-migration, high demand, and little opportunity for competition. In the project's immediate vicinity, there is little zoned land that can compete directly. In fact, we are in a unique and protected position that has lasted for decades and should last for many, many more years to come.

Some day we will sell Willowtree, but when we do I truly doubt the buyer will appreciate how rare the property is. Most buyers treat all cash flow the same. They use a cap rate that is a function of the property type. In fact, the difference in quality between the stream of income from a well-located, well-built, well-maintained property and the stream from an inconvenient or rundown property should be a lot higher than it is. In the case of Willowtree, we really have been blessed with an incredibly profitable property. It is a true cash cow.

Most buyers treat all cash flow the same. They use a cap rate that is a function of the property type. In fact, the difference in quality between the stream of income from a well-located, well-built, well-maintained property and the stream from an inconvenient or rundown property should be a lot higher than it is.

As I write this book and for the first time in quite a few years, despite its quality and all I have just said, we are considering selling Willowtree. During the first half of 2003, we have seen apartment properties sell at what we consider to be historically favorable cap rates. Given its consistent cash flow, however, we would have to receive quite a significant offer to actually go through with a sale.

Hall Office Park: A Long-Term Plan

Another type of property typically held longer than one cycle is one that you plan to develop. Larger-scale properties are often developed in multiple phases over time. Our 1989 land purchase in Frisco, Texas, originally included 175 acres. But after giving up a portion of it for the Dallas North Tollway extension that fell across one edge of the property, we ended up with a little over 160 acres that could be developed.

Timing the Real Estate Market

We invested a great deal of time thinking about and master planning this development. We knew we were going to be on the edge of two major thoroughfares in the heart of what we rightly believed would be one of the best growth areas in Texas. In 1997, eight years after purchasing the land, we broke ground on the first 100,000-square-foot office building. We watched the building come up in the middle of fields of sunflowers in an area that caused many friends of mine to think I had finally lost my mind. It was, according to most, so far north that we were no longer in Texas.

When we brought prospects out to see the construction progress on our first building, we had to bring them out in four-wheel-drive vehicles. And as our opening drew near, construction was begun on the service drives for what would ultimately be the Dallas North Tollway right at the entrance to our development. Even so, this first building was leased completely within six months from being opened, beating our original estimate of 15 months.

We planned to build four million square feet of office space that would include buildings of varying sizes. In analyzing the market and the long-term future, our hope was for a 12- to 15-year construction program. Including anticipated delays, from the time we purchased the property in 1989 to completion of the last of the 20 buildings, we were easily looking at a time period of more than 20 years.

In a project like this, our money is not made in the first building or two. In a sense they are almost loss leaders. So much infrastructure costs for roads and capital improvements are needed for a project from scratch that it takes several buildings before one starts making money. It's truly a long-term situation. Our advantage is that we paid little for the land relative to the use we're making of it. Ultimately, that should work toward very favorable returns. In 1989 we paid about $0.50 a square foot for the land. By today's standards in that area, even with the currently depressed office market, the land would be worth closer to $8 to $10 per square foot. But that's just the beginning of the upside we foresee.

Hold Some Properties Longer Than One Cycle

Part of our goal was to start with a large enough property to build a totally different concept for office space. Rather than selling the commodity of space, which most developers do, we wanted to enhance the real estate with a better environment and more services. Put simply, our goal was and is to redefine office space as people know it.

Rather than selling the commodity of space, which most developers do, we wanted to redefine office space as people know it.

At this point, we have eight buildings completed. We are continuing to sign new leases, even during the worst downturn in the Dallas market since the mid 1980s. In 2002, for instance, we leased over 300,000 square feet of office space, while the overall Dallas market had a net loss in lease space of over four million square feet. We were in the only submarket that had net leasing and were the only buildings of our type that accomplished such substantial leasing activity in the down market.

The way we did it was a combination of offering people great value and a much better product. Among other things, we have invested $10 million in sculpture and art for the property. In the front part of the office park, where many developers would put a restaurant or a gas station, we built a sculpture garden of artwork by living Texas artists, which can be seen from the highway. This sculpture garden is open to the public and represents the front door to the overall development. It indicates that we want to be a friendly approachable office community, in a quality environment that appreciates beauty, both natural and artistic.

We have invested $10 million in sculpture and art for the property. In the front part of the office park, we built a sculpture garden, which can be seen from the highway. We want to be a friendly approachable office community, in a quality environment that appreciates beauty, both natural and artistic.

Our property also includes a health club, running trails, lakes, landscaping, and numerous unusual services. Indeed, if you're having a stressful day, you can get a massage from the Hall Office Park masseuse. If you want food delivered to your desk, that's easily arranged.

Because of the long-term nature of our plans, this clearly is a property that we knew from day one we would hold for more than one cycle. Whether we'll hold it until the end, when the last buildings are built, or sell it sometime after it's substantially complete is something I don't know. Ultimately, it's a property that will have a high-quality income stream. We already are fortunate to have such tenants as General Electric Credit Corporation, Fujitsu Transaction Solutions, and other major corporate tenants. We have no plans to sell this property in the near future and already are benefiting from our long-term management action plan. We also are tailoring our financing and other plans to hold for the longer term.

Don't let the scope of this example sway you from potentially trying this approach yourself. Many developments can be undertaken on a small scale on a smaller property and be highly successful.

Reasons to Hold for More Than One Cycle

There are two primary reasons to hold Willowtree and Hall Office Park for more than one cycle: Willowtree is a unique property and Hall Office Park is a development property with long-term management action plans.

Unique properties like Willowtree often can and should be held for periods longer than one cycle. Usually these properties are in areas with barriers to entry or have other unique features.

One example is the Chicago Merchandise Mart, which was owned by the Kennedy family for many years, over a number of cycles. In my opinion, they held the property for all the right reasons. It is unique and, like Willowtree, provided a good, high-quality, stable cash flow. It had a special and particular use in an ideal location.

Hold Some Properties Longer Than One Cycle

If your property is so special that others can't compete with it, you would certainly want to look hard at holding it for the long-term. If your property is also physically sound, that's another important reason to consider holding.

Projects such as Hall Office Park require multiple cycles to realize their full potential. Other developments of less magnitude still could take at least two cycles to complete. Many developments can be completed within one cycle, but may take multiple cycles to realize their full value. This also varies depending on when in the cycle the project is complete.

Creating value through a positive history of operations can do much to increase pricing at the time of sale. The idea is to sell at the most positive time of the cycle—whether you hold for one cycle or more.

Quality of Construction Is Important

Despite whatever money you spend on initial improvements to an acquired property, each and every day properties suffer from wear and tear and they depreciate. You'll always wish you had more reserves.

Holding a property beyond one cycle increases the risk from deferred maintenance. Therefore, if you intend to hold the property longer, for whatever reason, it's important that it be well built. In the case of the Hall Office Park buildings, we're the developer and owner and we know they're built to last for many, many years in top condition with minimum maintenance. That may cost more up front, but that's key to a long-term strategy.

Holding a property beyond one cycle increases the risk from deferred maintenance. Therefore, if you intend to hold the property longer, it's important that it be well built.

Location Is Critical

One cycle is easier to see than multiple cycles. Looking ahead, it's important that demand be steady and, if possible, increasing for your market area. In-migration and new job growth are both good indicators to look for that will increase demand for your location.

Also consider any planned improvements to the infrastructure of the area. For instance, knowing that a north-south toll road was coming past a major east-west thoroughfare in Frisco told us that Hall Office Park had a good long-term future with better infrastructure to come. Similarly you should look to other positives, such as proximity to an airport, a new port, and highway construction or other factors that will increase access. Location is not just a static place but an ongoing dynamic consideration. So look at all of the things that will be coming up in future years in your particular area and assess how they will impact your property.

On the negative side, consider possible new competition. How much nearby land is zoned for the same type of product you have? What is the price of that land? Will you have new competition that will make your product just another commodity?

The ultimate goal if you plan to hold for more than one cycle is to have a property in a location and at a price level and overall financing structure that provides it with a unique position in the marketplace. You want a property that can't be duplicated in a market. This is the goal: to one way or another feel secure that no other property can compete directly. Understanding plans for the future rather than the current conditions is critical to your decision.

The ultimate goal if you plan to hold for more than one cycle is to have a property with a unique position in the marketplace. You want a property that can't be duplicated in a market.

How Financing Figures into Holding for More Than One Cycle

Another thing about which you need to be thoughtful is how your property is financed. If you are holding a property for more than one cycle, when opportunities present themselves, try to secure more favorable, long-term financing. On the other hand, if you are making improvements in your property and you believe the value will be going up, a shorter loan that can be refinanced as the property value increases could be a more attractive alternative.

Often when you hold properties for multiple cycles, you can refinance the property and actually take out a lot of your original investment—in some cases even more than you invested. Properties like Willowtree that we have owned many years have been refinanced multiple times. Each time, we have taken money out of the property, recapturing investment and then some.

It's important to realize that each time you refinance and take money out of a property, it isn't a taxable event. That's money that you can use for other investment purposes and you don't have to pay taxes on it at the time of your refinancing. This is a great opportunity and one more important benefit of holding properties for more than one cycle.

Part
Five

When to Sell

Selling Basics

There will always be a better time to sell than the day you actually do. But real estate isn't a science; it's an art, which means it's subjective. Within most markets, you try to find a pocket of selling opportunity. When you've determined it's time to sell, to do so successfully, start by thinking like a buyer.

Buyers will pay more for properties that look good. Fresh paint and new carpet are some of the best improvements you can make when preparing to sell. As with everything else I've told you, there are exceptions and a certain fundamental psychology goes along with this particular concept. Some buyers will not appreciate what you've just done to fix up your property. They are instead considering what they can do to make it better and, of course, different from whatever it is that you've just done. The same is true for your operating results. While you may be proud to show off what a great job you've done running the property, the buyer will be contemplating how he or she will do things better.

One of the great wonders of our economic system is that optimism abounds. Most buyers have a plan and are pretty certain they can improve on your performance. Whatever you do, don't begrudge potential buyers this attitude. Encourage them and their vision. While you're at it, go ahead and admit that you probably haven't done everything you could have done to maximize the property's value. In the end, a buyer's optimism can help you get a higher price than your numbers might otherwise justify.

One of the great wonders of our economic system is that optimism abounds. A buyer's optimism can help you get a higher price than your numbers might otherwise justify.

Besides, in many cases, the buyer is right. We have sold many properties to other owners who have done a better job with them than we were doing. Sometimes owners hold properties too long and begin to overlook opportunities for improvement. Management can get stale even with the best talent and intentions. New ideas and new people are good for real estate properties. It takes new perspectives to make new things happen.

So, how do you find a prospective buyer to encourage? And when you find them, how do you negotiate and structure the sale? These are important questions and fundamental to the overall process of timing your real estate transactions.

Think Through Your Property's Position in the Timing Cycle

When considering whether or not to sell a particular property, just like when considering whether or not to buy one, you need to consider the property's position in the timing cycle. Revisit the processes described in Chapters 6 and 7 to establish this, with the goal to start the sales process in the later stages of an upward cycle.

As will become clearer in this chapter, selling property
consuming process. Because of this, it's important to start u.
during the upward cycle and not get greedy trying to wait for the
highest prices at the top of the market. Rarely does anyone hit the
exact top except by accident.

It's important to start the sale during the upward cycle and not get
greedy trying to wait for the highest prices at the top of the market.

Determine Your Goals

When you're selling a property, it's important to think about how much
money you want for your property, but also, more importantly, how
much you think you can actually get. What's the lowest price you are
willing to accept? Take a look at comparable sales in your area to be
realistic. A combination of applying a cap rate to your NOI and looking
at this comparable data can help you determine an asking price.

One of the ways we determine asking price is to interview real
estate brokers. If we're going to have a broker represent us in our
property sale, which is often the case, it's fair to ask several of them
how they would price the property and what they think the high and
low sale range should be. With anecdotal information on cap rates,
input from the brokerage community, and your own general understanding of the market, you should be able to come to a reasonable
and final decision on pricing.

Set your sales price at 10% to 15% higher than you actually would
accept.

You will not want to set your price so high that you scare away
bidders. You don't want to set it so low that you leave money on the
table either. You should set your sales price at 10% to 15% higher
than you actually would accept.

Price isn't the only goal you need to think about. Do you want to sell for cash only? Or would you be willing to take part of your money in the form of a promissory note secured by the property through a second mortgage? What are your timing considerations? Would you take a lower price for a quick sale? If so, what kind of discount would that be worth to you?

These are the kinds of tradeoffs that will eventually come up and require fairly quick decisions. It's best to think through as many as you can in advance—before you reach a critical moment and have only a short time to respond. Pricing, timing needs, cash or financing: these are all things that you should have firmly in your mind before you proceed.

The Value of Real Estate Brokers

Because of our experience and history negotiating complex transactions, we are able to negotiate our own sales in many market areas without the assistance of a broker. But this is an exception and not the norm.

Having a professional real estate broker is normally a critical ingredient for a successful outcome. Brokers provide exposure, attract qualified buyers, and bring market- and property-specific knowledge to the table. It's also helpful to have a negotiating intermediary to facilitate getting the deal done. With the vast majority of our purchases and sales, we retain and rely on experienced real estate brokers.

A professional real estate broker is normally a critical ingredient for a successful outcome.

NEGOTIATE THE BROKERAGE FEE

Decades ago, when I started out in this business, every transaction came with a 6% real estate brokerage fee. This 6% of the sales price often was split between a buyer's broker and a seller's broker, or even among several brokers who were working on behalf of one or the other party in the deal. It wasn't fashionable then to negotiate the brokers' commission percentages. But, over the years, establishing specific commissions for each transaction has become an accepted part of the negotiation process.

Traditionally, the smaller the deal, the larger the commission percentage. For single-family homes or small rental properties, commissions often range from 4% to 5%. Commissions on larger transactions can often be as low as 1% or even less. Routinely paying a 6% commission today without consideration for size, complexity of the transaction, etc., would be out of step with the norm.

DETERMINE A MARKETING PLAN

Negotiating the commission is just one part of the written contractual understanding you must have with your real estate broker. You need to know how the broker plans to market the property.

Who are the targeted potential buyers? Will he or she advertise for you? How much money does he or she intend to spend on advertising and in what media—Internet, newspapers, trade magazines, billboards? If a major brokerage firm is retained, who will be your daily point of contact? These are all questions you need to ask before entering into an agreement with a broker.

Look for 1031 Exchange Buyers, if Possible

Internal Revenue Code Section 1031 allows sellers of real estate to exchange properties on a tax-free basis for other real estate. In simplistic terms, the current law permits a 45-day period during which a seller can identify and name the potential properties that would be exchanged. From the date of the property sale, the seller then has another 180 days to complete the "exchange."

A 1031 exchange buyer is highly motivated. These buyers have the money and are working against the clock. They certainly don't want to lose their tax-savings opportunity. For all these reasons, 1031 tax-free exchange buyers should be a targeted part of your marketing plan.

As you'll see later in this chapter, you will have your own income tax considerations when you sell. These should also cause you to personally consider the benefits associated with a 1031 exchange. For many, this is a good option.

Methods of Selling

There are a variety of methods you and real estate brokers and agents can use to move property. We will explore those here.

THE "MULTIPLE LISTING" APPROACH

A fundamental approach to selling real estate is through multiple listing services. All real estate brokers and agents within a property's market area receive these listings, which include property photography and statistics, on a regular basis. Getting the word out to the brokerage community is key, but for larger properties different approaches may be more appropriate. Brokers and buyers of significant portfolios and notable properties can be all over the world, so limiting your activity to one local market's multiple listing service may not provide sufficient exposure.

THE "AUCTION" METHOD

For medium- and larger-sized investment properties, auctions have become an effective method of selling. Using this method presupposes a high level of investor interest in the property.

Auctions typically are handled by brokers, who fuel the competitive buying process by using multiple methods of generating exposure during a 45- to 60-day period. These include regional and national advertising, direct mail, e-mail, listings on the Internet, and targeted personalized mailings to qualified prospects. Those interested in the purchase have a date by which they must respond with a letter of intent in order to continue the negotiation process. After that date, generally no future inquiries are accepted.

Once letters of intent are received, a limited number of prospective buyers are then given another 30 to 45 days to analyze the property. These three to six "finalists" have an opportunity to get all their questions answered and then come to the table with their "best and final" offer. The broker uses this time to set expectations and let the prospective purchasers know what you, as a seller, might be willing to accept. These prospective buyers have generally all made close offers in their original letters of intent and know that, in order to win, they are going to have to increase their initial offers.

On the date the "best and final" offers are due, one buyer is selected. Sometimes a second buyer may be chosen to make a back-up offer. At this point, sales agreements are executed and the 30- to 60-day due diligence period begins. After due diligence, another 15 to 45 days are allowed for closing.

Selling a property this way takes time—usually four to eight months—with possible extensions negotiated after the due diligence phase to allow the buyer additional time to arrange financing.

PRICING PROPERTIES VS. OPEN-ENDED BIDS

We have sold properties without ever setting a price and started negotiating from an initial offer. But it's more common for sellers to establish the price they would be willing to take for the property in advance.

In a frenzied "seller's market," utilizing the auction process to receive open-ended bids can and does work. If, for example, you owned a rental condominium in a hot area in which people are willing to pay a premium, an open-ended bid process might be a good way to maximize the property sale price to you. There may be a minimum offer required in order to participate in the process. The seller always has the right to withdraw the property. The key is to determine whether the price should be established up front or left open-ended. Because properties and markets vary extensively, a decision about trying to get open-ended bids should be made with the counsel of an experienced real estate broker.

Consider the Buyer's Financing Needs

Part of being a successful seller is thinking about the needs of the buyer. Do you want all cash? Will new financing be required? If so, you can help facilitate the sale by locating sources of funding for buyers to pursue. At a minimum, get as many of the reports required by lenders ready as early as possible to facilitate this part of the process.

Part of being a successful seller is thinking about the needs of the buyer.

If you are selling a property with an existing loan, check with your lender to see what is required to enable a buyer to assume your loan. Sometimes the loan assumption process can be extremely time-consuming and problematic. But if you can work through these details in advance, you'll be better prepared to expedite the process toward a smooth closing.

Under special circumstances, you may have to help locate other, nontraditional sources of funding, such as mezzanine financing, to help the buyer close the gap between their mortgage and the purchase price in order to reduce the down payment. Also consider whether or not you would be willing to hold a second mortgage on the property yourself. Letting potential buyers know about available financing before they make an offer will help keep your property price at a higher level.

In sum, the financing component of a sale depends on the specific property and the lending environment. Still, advance preparation to provide financing options to potential buyers can increase the purchase price you'll receive and expedite the sales process.

Before You Sell, Order Reports on Your Property

Lenders require certain reports at the time of sale. Starting on these early can be to your advantage. Ordering environmental and engineering reports and surveys before you even have a buyer can help save time and make the due diligence process easier. It's even better to order these reports before you begin marketing your property. Any relevant information you receive then can be made available to your prospective buyers.

Full disclosure is the best practice. You should never hold back on information. You will only open yourself up to significant liabilities if you fail to disclose facts about your property.

Marketing and Maximizing Exposure

It usually takes 45 to 60 days to adequately market a property. Larger, complicated commercial properties can take six months to market properly. Organize your marketing plan before you sign a listing agreement with a broker. Talk to local title companies and find out how to reach 1031 tax-free exchange buyers. Think about how to get exposure and which advertising mediums will be most effective for your property. *The Wall Street Journal, Barron's,* and other publications with large circulations are appropriate for high-end properties. In advance of signing a brokerage listing agreement, negotiate to ensure that the real estate broker retained to sell your property pays for the advertising.

Analyzing Letters of Intent

Your real estate broker should be out talking with prospective buyers and encouraging them to turn in their letters of intent. A good broker will make sure that these letters are similar in format and that all points are clearly made.

It's good to find out as much as you can about the potential buyers. Know who they are. Ask for references. Make phone calls. Qualify these prospects and check their credibility. It's important to be able to trust what they say as you approach the closing table.

The Legal Process

There are numerous laws covering the transferral of real estate that you need to be aware of, and a good attorney can be your best friend sometimes.

PICKING YOUR LAWYER

Seek the advice of an attorney at the beginning of the sales process. Make your expectations clear, as lawyers can function in a variety of roles.

I believe attorneys are best used to handle the closing and negotiate the legal points of your contract. Good legal advice is paramount, but having attorneys get too involved in other ways actually can be harmful to a transaction. Even the best-intentioned can be deal-killers. They can be too conservative or focus only on everything that can go wrong. You don't want to over-negotiate to the point that a good deal falls apart due to a buyer's frustration with your attorney.

Attorneys are best used to handle the closing and negotiate the legal points of your contract. Having attorneys get too involved in other ways actually can be harmful to a transaction.

ENTERING INTO THE SALES AGREEMENT

Once you get past the letter of intent stage, you move on to the "best and final" offers stage. It's time to negotiate the sales agreement.

We always prepare a sales agreement in familiar format so that we can easily execute it. We send these to the buyers in advance and tell them to return them as part of their "best and final" offer. At this point, they can let us know what they would like to change in our standard agreement. This gives us the opportunity to know where we stand on key issues and the ability to forecast the likelihood of actually closing the deal.

NEGOTIATING THE CONTRACT

Make sure your contracts and agreements are fair. If they are too one-sided, you will turn buyers off by being too tough from the beginning. Don't take a shortsighted approach. Be reasonable and pursue a win-win scenario. We modify portions of our standard agreements if appropriate, but we also create contracts that we would not hesitate to sign if we were the buyers.

Be reasonable and pursue a win-win scenario.

No two attorneys would ever write a contract the same way, so you can expect language changes in any agreement. It is our position, though, to avoid making changes unless there are good reasons for doing so.

The sales contract should address clearly all major points in the sale. Your attorney will guide you through the sale contract terms, but a few key issues are worth mentioning here.

One thing a contract should discuss is the length of the due diligence phase. Generally, it should be a 45- to 60-day period, with closing taking place 15 to 30 days thereafter.

Another issue that the contract to purchase should discuss is exactly who pays what at the time of closing. These issues are called "prorations" and they can be paid by either the buyer or the seller. Our view on prorations is that they should be reasonable and customary. We don't try to gouge buyers and we don't expect them to try to gouge us. Prorations are used in cases when the seller has paid for something that will benefit the buyer after the property changes hands. An example is property taxes, which the seller may have already paid, but for which the benefit might last for another six months after the buyer takes over. The buyer at closing would pay the amount of the property taxes that applies to any time after the sale date. Similarly, insurance could be prepaid. Utilities are often read on meters up to the date of closing, but sometimes utilities are prepaid or are owed later. Rents are sometimes prepaid and sometimes they are delinquent. The general theory of proration is that the seller gets the benefit and burden up to the day of closing and the buyer gets the benefit and burden thereafter.

This is the small stuff, so don't sweat it. Don't think small. How you negotiate an agreement sets a standard that can come back to haunt you.

Don't think small. How you negotiate an agreement sets a standard that can come back to haunt you.

The most contentious area when negotiating sales agreements is the seller's warranties. Buyers' attorneys will want you to warrant conditions and a variety of other aspects of the property. Sellers' attorneys will want you to warrant nothing.

We generally shoot for selling our properties "as is and where is"—in other words, without much of a warranty. We will, however, provide warranties that to the best of our knowledge and information we are disclosing everything we know about the property. We are not in the business of creating situations where we will be involved in lawsuits down the line. We also are not an insurance company for the buyer's future needs.

DEFENDING YOUR GOAL

Keep in mind that once you've entered into a sales agreement, from that point forward everything you do as a seller is "defending your goal." You are no different from a goalie in a hockey game. You are simply defending your goal and trying to keep the other side from changing the score.

As a seller, once you have signed the sales agreement, things won't get better. A buyer won't go through due diligence and then tell you he or she has decided to pay you more money, but a buyer will let you know all the reasons he or she would like to pay less. A buyer's goal may be to buy the property, but a strategy toward that goal is to whittle away at the price. Expect buyers to rationalize a lower price.

SURVIVING DUE DILIGENCE—A GENERAL POINT

Defending your position is what due diligence is all about. During due diligence, you're providing the buyer evidence of how your property has been performing and why. As the seller, you're trying to keep the contract intact without a reduction in price and you should provide full and accurate information about the property as required in your contract.

Create a general atmosphere of competition. Have another buyer in the wings and let your primary buyer know about him or her.

One way to survive the due diligence period without a reduction in price is to create a general atmosphere of competition. Have another buyer in the wings and let your primary buyer know about him or her. Sometimes there even may be multiple offers. Your backup buyer may want to proceed with due diligence on your property. You often will have to foot the bill for these costs because this isn't the primary buyer, but the psychology associated with doing so can often work to your benefit. Having a backup offer lets the first buyer know that trying to renegotiate could kill the deal.

RETRADING THE DEAL

By qualifying buyers in advance, we try to avoid those who are likely to renegotiate or "retrade" before entering into an agreement.

Retrading means using flimsy excuses to lower the purchase price. Many buyers offer a price they have no intention of paying and then look for any reason to lower the offer during due diligence.

As a buyer, we don't believe in retrading as a buying strategy. We'll do so only when facts are substantially different from what we expected and would cause us to otherwise walk away from the deal entirely. There have been times, for example, when we have reviewed land purchases and found that our original plans to subdivide the property wouldn't work. We discuss what we have found with the seller and propose new terms. If the deal doesn't work, at least the seller has received more information on the property and we hopefully are able to part company on friendly terms.

CLOSING THE TRANSACTION

After all you go through, closing can be very anticlimactic. It takes so much to get to that table that when you finally do, you often let the process happen through attorneys or through the mail. Final closings occur at the title company, but they can happen with or without your physical presence.

As we discussed in Chapter 8, the title company is really the coordinator for all of the closing work. It produces the closing statement, which handles all of the prorations as well as distribution of funds. Typically the title company has held the earnest money in escrow during due diligence. At the time of the closing, the title company will receive from the buyer a certified check, a cashier's check, or wired funds and handle the disbursements to pay off any existing loan, fund a new mortgage, or do whatever else needs to be done to complete the transaction.

My recommendation—which by the way is advice I don't personally follow—is to take time to celebrate. Acknowledge the process and those who worked so hard to complete the deal. It's no small feat to let go of a property you've owned and perhaps managed for a long time. So, take the time to celebrate—you deserve it.

Income Taxes Relating to Property Sales

With the exception of 1031 tax-free exchanges and the possible exception for a primary residence, when you sell a piece of property you will owe federal income tax. You may also owe a state income tax and a tax that relates to property sales. Some states have transfer fees. You should look into taxes ahead of time so that you're not surprised.

When it comes to federal income taxes, real estate has some favorable features. During the time of your ownership, you are allowed to depreciate the property and take losses on paper that are not actually cash losses. Paper losses combined with any actual tax losses can be used to offset income from other real estate under the passive activity rule. If you are an active real estate investor and classified as a real estate professional, these losses also can be applied against real estate income you may receive. (The qualifications for this are fairly detailed and you need to consult a tax advisor.) In general, though, there are great tax benefits during the time of your ownership. Sometimes, if you cannot use the losses, you can hold them for use at a later time. These suspended losses may be available for use when you sell the property.

When you sell a property, you will pay taxes based upon what is called your "tax basis." The tax basis adjusts each year, based on the original cost minus the tax losses that you have taken along the way. People tend to forget that they have had benefits along the way and then they are surprised when they have a tax basis that is significantly below what their mortgage might be. This happens particularly when you have owned a property for an extended time and refinanced it at a higher level than your original mortgage. In worst-case situations, you can actually end up with taxable gain and not enough cash to pay the tax. Although hopefully it will never be an issue for you, but even a foreclosure is treated as a sale.

Without getting into exhaustive detail, there is one other major benefit that real estate has over some other investments: the vast proportion of real estate properties will be held for over a year and will be taxed at long-term capital gain rates. These rates are more favorable than regular income tax rates, with the maximum now being 15% of the gain.

Be aware that under current law, a portion of the gain on depreciable real property upon the sale may be taxable at 25% for unrecaptured depreciation. Even though you are paying a tax when you sell, you have actually saved taxes while you owned the property, so the taxing structure really is reasonable overall.

1031 Exchanges

Section 1031 of the Internal Revenue Code provides an opportune way to delay taxes at the time of sale. This provision allows for tax-free exchanges of similar types of property. If you want to pursue this approach, which many real estate investors do, your best bet is to find an intermediary known as a tax-free exchanger. Your lawyer or title company can find these intermediaries easily for you. For remarkably low fees (often in the range of $300-$400 for the entire transaction), the intermediary will provide the documents and explain the process.

A summary of a 1031 exchange may help here. You'll have to put the money you get from the sale in escrow. Then you'll have 45 days to identify another piece of real estate that you intend to buy using the money. In order to avoid taxes, you would have to match up your equity and debt so that the new property had at least the same amount of debt and the same amount of equity as the property that you are selling. You have a total of 180 days to close on your new purchase. You typically want to identify more than one property in case one falls through. If you don't plan to invest in another piece of real estate, Section 1031 won't benefit you.

What I find difficult about 1031 exchanges is that you have a relatively short time frame in which to find one or more properties to exchange. The decision to exchange often puts buyers in a position where they are so concerned about paying taxes that they overpay for a new property. Always consider whether you're paying too much for your new property. Don't let taxes drive your deal. My advice is to be cautious about the pressures that 1031 exchanges can bring to bear; don't sacrifice your standards for a property and end up purchasing a property just to avoid paying taxes.

The decision to exchange often puts buyers in a position where they are so concerned about paying taxes that they overpay for a new property. ... Don't let taxes drive your deal.

Three Bottom-Line Reflections on Selling

1. **It's a long process; don't underestimate it.** With rare exceptions, from start to finish, selling investment properties generally takes four to eight months.

2. **It's an uncertain process.** Unlike stock prices, we have no daily quotes for real estate. Terms and timing of transactions are unknowns.

3. **How you handle the process can make a big difference in the result.** There's no question in my mind that managing the process in a way that seeks a win-win outcome for both the buyer and the seller will work more to your advantage than trying to wring every last dollar out of the buyer.

It's Better to Be Too Early Than Too Late

Markets are always changing. Timing the start of your sales process is paramount.

In 2002, I saw a great opportunity. Interest rates were coming down and the stock market had been off for the third year in a row. Money was flowing into real estate and prices were pushing higher than what made sense. We knew that properties were experiencing declining operating results, but despite that, we saw prices going up anyway. Newspaper articles were being written about office building prices rising and we knew this was happening even more so with apartment buildings.

We decided to package a large number of apartment properties and put them up for sale. But we went about it slowly and started late. This was a mistake. Our timing was thrown off, and, by the time our properties were marketed, the real estate investment climate had changed.

During that same time period, I saw buyers walk away from several significant deals that had been under contract. Cycles shift quickly and dramatically and cannot always be predicted.

I don't consider myself an expert at selling. It is something that I have to continually work at. I think many real estate entrepreneurs find it a lot more fun to be buyers and owners than to be sellers. It feels to me like I'm sacrificing something when I sell a property. At the same time, it's a critical part of the overall process of ultimately being profitable in real estate.

When the Pay Window Is Open, Sell: The "Sell When Everyone Wants It" Strategy

T he "Sell When Everyone Wants It" approach is in many ways the opposite of the "Buy When There's Blood in the Streets" approach. The two together make up the contrarian approach to real estate investing.

As you have learned, the contrarian approach is to buy when everyone else is selling out of fear or desperation—and then to sell when everyone else is buying aggressively. In a booming real estate market, most investors optimistically believe prices are going to continue moving higher and higher—and at times they will move up to unsustainable heights. This is a great time to sell.

Gates of Arlington: The Pay Window Was Open ...

Years ago, a seasoned lawyer said to me, "When the pay window is open, hit the bid." What he was trying to teach this young real estate investor who was never ready to sell was to recognize when it is time to reap the rewards of hard work. *When someone else wants something you've got, and they want it badly enough, let them have it.*

The following story is about a recent apartment sale that we had not planned. The property was not on the market or listed "for sale." But once we received that initial offer and others heard that the property might be available, we began to receive higher and higher offers.

The Gates of Arlington is a 465-unit apartment development in Arlington County, Virginia. It is attractive and well built, but also 60 years old and far from maintenance-free. We had owned the property for 18 years when, in the spring of 2002, we were approached by a group of local real estate brokers with a client interested in buying. We don't often respond to unsolicited calls such as these, because they are typically not productive. But in this instance we were intrigued enough to start a dialogue, even though we weren't really in the market to sell. After several preliminary discussions, we found ourselves seriously considering accepting a $27 million offer.

A LITTLE PUBLICITY MAKES A BIG DIFFERENCE

To our initial surprise and disappointment, the local newspapers got wind of the discussions and broke the news that the Gates of Arlington might be sold. The article created quite a stir, because Arlington County has very little affordable housing for average working people. Much of the multifamily property in the area had already been converted to high-priced, for-sale condominiums. Because our property had smaller apartment units and had been around for so many years without being converted to condominiums, it was one of the last large affordable places to live in the county.

For these reasons, we were concerned that the media attention would ultimately derail our ability to sell the property. As it turned out, the media attention actually generated additional calls from brokers representing other buyers interested in the property.

In particular, two very credible offers came from real estate investment trusts (REITs). One of them wanted to buy the property and then build additional units on the vacant land that was part of the property. Even Arlington County voiced a buying interest, motivated to preserve the property as affordable housing. County officials began to call me detailing their plan for us to sell to a non-profit business that they would back financially. A local congressman wrote me a letter endorsing the Arlington County plan. Even friends of friends from the State Department were contacting me. The pressure was intense.

Weeks went by, with offers inching higher and higher among the bidders. Finally, through multiple discussions, we decided on a price I threw out as acceptable: $35.5 million. This was $8.5 million higher than the offer that caused us to consider selling in the first place. The county and its non-profit agreed to pay the $35.5 million.

Rather than trying to get an even higher price from another buyer whose plans for the property might be in conflict with the county, we decided to accept the offer and move forward with the county non-profit as the buyer. Ironically, even from this point forward, the deal didn't proceed as smoothly as we had hoped.

BUMPS IN THE ROAD

Every real estate sale has its own unique life span and its own difficulties. Selling is never as simple or as easy in reality as it appears to be on paper or in most how-to books.

Every real estate sale has its own unique life span and its own difficulties.

The Gates of Arlington went under contract with AHC, Inc., the Arlington County non-profit, in May of 2002. AHC, Inc. was to pay $14.5 million in cash and assume an existing $21 million first mortgage loan that we had just obtained by refinancing the property with a 7% mortgage. The county could borrow at lower rates, but to prepay our new mortgage so soon was cost-prohibitive.

Closing was delayed many times as we continued to deal with a wide range of issues with the non-profit and the county. The deal structure had to be approved by two rating agencies as well as various layers of lenders. It all became immensely time-consuming and complex. Over a period of six months, we gave eight contract extensions to AHC, Inc. just to keep the transaction alive. It was a disappointing and frustrating time in that we had passed on other potential buyers who could have closed much faster and who were willing to pay the same purchase price.

At one particularly trying time during the process, we went back to talk with some of the other potential buyers. We discovered that the market had changed. Their original aggressive interest had waned and none were willing to come close to paying $35.5 million. Had we contracted with one of them earlier in the spring, however, we might have been able to close in 60 or 90 days. But as time continued to pass, we found ourselves with no alternative to AHC. The good news about this was that, on a personal level, I wanted AHC to succeed. I liked the idea of preserving the property as affordable housing for Arlington County.

We discovered that the market had changed. Their original aggressive interest had waned…. As time continued to pass, we found ourselves with no alternative.

Finally after much hand-holding, the transaction closed on November 27 (my wedding anniversary). My wife and I were in Paris working on the renovations of our two hotels there when I received word. We wish AHC, Inc. and Arlington County well with their acquisition and hope the property becomes even more valuable in the future.

Had I been younger and less sophisticated, I might have become greedier about the Gates of Arlington. Since we weren't considering selling at the time we got that first offer, I might have tried to hold onto it longer. But, as it turned out, we understood what was meant by "when the pay window is open, hit the bid." We sold the Gates of Arlington for a capitalization rate of 6%, extremely low from a historical standpoint. It's an older property with high maintenance costs and repetitive deferred maintenance, so the effective cap rate after deducting for these higher expenses probably was closer to 5%.

SOMETIMES YOU WIN, SOMETIMES YOU LOSE

Part of what I know about selling comes from making mistakes and missing the market. We purchased the Gates of Arlington as part of a larger acquisition we made in 1983 that included a sister property with 980 apartment units. In the mid 1980s, even in Arlington County, well-located property was suffering. Our net income on both of these properties was significantly lower than the loan payments. Vacancies were high, rental rates were low, and interest rates on our loans were high. It was a deadly combination.

Part of what I know about selling comes from making mistakes and missing the market.

The Gates of Arlington and its sister property had different lenders. We began trying to work out payment plans with each one, but we lost the sister property to foreclosure. We were able to reach an agreement with the Gates of Arlington lender that allowed us to continue operating through the downturn.

Now, fast-forward to 2002, when the Gates of Arlington became a big winner for everyone involved. This was possible because we had been able to reach a mortgage modification agreement with the Gates of Arlington lender when we had financial problems many years earlier.

With real estate, the key is to hang on until the timing is right. It's all about timing.

Selling Doesn't Just Happen

The Gates of Arlington was an exception. The reality is that an unsolicited call rarely leads to a sale. The process of selling real estate is one that is best accomplished in a clear, thoughtful manner and is directed by the seller, not the buyer. There are many decisions to be made about selling that will vary by property type, timing, location, etc. But there are also some global rules about selling worth considering.

It's Hard to Sell When Everything's Right— But Just Do It!

It's a "seller's market" when everyone wants to buy your property. But more often than not, because they want it, you won't want to sell it. Ironically, there is a psychological block about selling something at the top. Everybody wants to hold on, waiting for even higher peaks. Perhaps we get emotionally attached to our property or perhaps we just think that, if things are going this well, they are only going to get better.

It's unreasonable to think that anyone can tell what the top is until history shows it to us. Hindsight is the best judge of tops and bottoms. At the same time, we all can tell when prices have reached very high levels. As with the stock market in January and February of 2000, investors believed that the profitable situation would just keep getting better. Very few were getting out of the stock market by taking their profits in early 2000. And just a few months later when the NASDAQ crashed, emotions changed quickly.

It's unreasonable to think that anyone can tell what the top is until history shows it to us. Hindsight is the best judge of tops and bottoms.

Overstaying your welcome in real estate can be just like it was for those who played too long in the NASDAQ. Things can go from very good to very bad in what seems like an instant. Getting out at what feels like a high point, even if you think you are leaving something on the table, is the right way to go.

Four Ways to Know It's a Seller's Market

1. **You can feel it.** If you're active in the marketplace, you will feel the turn in favor of the seller and know the market is at a high point. After some years in the business, it's not difficult to know when things are booming. The real question is if you will have the courage to get out in time or if greed will keep you in too long.

2. **Market data doesn't lie.** You can always get market data from title companies and real estate brokers. The facts are all right there for you to analyze. Are prices going up? How much, how high, how fast?

3. **Listen to others.** Anecdotal information from other owners and from real estate brokers can help point out the top. What do brokers say? Is the market dangerously high?

4. **Sometimes you'll know because it simply falls on you.** When we received those calls from brokers with multiple clients wanting to buy the Gates of Arlington, and then the newspaper article hit, and then even the county was chasing us, we would have been crazy to miss the obvious clues that we were in a seller's market.

Create a Bidding War

When you are in a seller's market, use the techniques described in Chapter 14 whenever possible to control the process. In particular, push for a dynamic that will create some friction between two or three buyers and start a bidding war, especially in that best and final round process.

But don't push too far and lose them all. Just let each one know that they have some credible competition. That piece of honest information will begin to work for you. You will need to develop your own intuition about how much you can push—remembering that pushing too far can backfire on you.

Timing Is Critical: Don't Miss Your Window

Just like you can get too greedy in the negotiation process, you can get too greedy by waiting too long. In 2002, with the Gates of Arlington as our clue, we realized we were clearly in a seller's market. Prices were escalating rapidly. We made plans to package and sell some of our other properties as a group, which takes a little longer than selling one at a time. But we made the mistake of waiting too long. We didn't expect the market to change so quickly, but it did. Suddenly apartment operations were going downhill at the same time prices were rising because of lower interest rates. In the end, the market corrected itself by slowing down and stalling virtually all transactions in late 2002.

The lesson here is that, when the window is open, go for the deal. For all we might say that's positive about real estate, the fact is that it's not a very liquid asset. The market can turn on a dime, so be aggressive about carrying out your selling strategy. Once you've made a decision, act on it!

16

When Positive Momentum Is at Risk, Get Out: The "Sell Before Prices Go Down Again" Strategy

The "Sell Before Prices Go Down Again" strategy is the second of the major sell strategies. The previous chapter noted that a good "sell" indicator is the presence of lots of buyers for your property. This chapter looks at another "sell" indicator: a decline in the positive momentum and general enthusiasm in the market where your property is located.

More often than not, the point of maximum enthusiasm among investors about a real estate market indicates the top of the cycle. If you are thinking strategically about timing the real estate market and you have learned to read the signs and trends, you will be in a better position than most investors to spot the earliest indications that the momentum is stopping and take your profits. In this chapter, you will learn how to time your sale by selling before the market turns down again.

What Is Positive Momentum?

When you're experiencing a period of positive momentum and there is a general sense that things are moving upward, usually NOI is also moving up. With office space, for instance, there is a general perception that rental rates and occupancies will rise and, therefore, NOI will rise, too. Similarly, this momentum means property prices should also rise, due in part to lower cap rates as buyers are more aggressively interested in particular types of real estate in different locations. The rising prices are also a reflection of the higher NOIs and improving operations.

The timing, degree, and speed of positive momentum all vary from cycle to cycle. There is no common thread to predicting how strong the upward momentum will be or how long it will continue. Each situation must be analyzed individually with consideration given to all of the relevant facts.

There is no common thread to predicting how strong the upward momentum will be or how long it will continue.

The following story describes how we purchased and sold two office towers in downtown Dallas—and a real-life example of how to sell when positive momentum is at risk.

Catching the Wave

For much of the late 1980s and early 1990s, downtown Dallas had the dubious distinction of having one of the worst downtown office markets in the country. Vacancies had been at or near 30% for so long that developers had stopped building altogether.

In October of 1994, an interesting building known as St. Paul Place came on the market. It was one of the newest properties in downtown, even though it had been completed in 1987. The Bank of Montreal had foreclosed on the building and was ready to sell.

The "Sell Before Prices Go Down Again" Strategy

The 375,000-square-foot, 22-story green glass office building was small by most downtown standards, but it was still one of the last modern high rises to be built and had some distinct advantages. First, its location in the heart of downtown on Ross Avenue is ideal, right alongside a number of other office buildings and directly across the street from the Dallas Museum of Art. Another advantage was that it has uniquely shaped small floors that were flexible for tenants of different sizes. Overall, it was a nice, high-end building.

We were one of 14 prospective bidders when the bank put St. Paul Place up for sale. In and of itself, that was an extraordinary number of bidders, considering that it had been many years since any of the modern high rises in Dallas had changed hands. Our company was different from the other bidders, though, in that we were willing to pay cash and close within a very short time. After pursuing a couple of the other higher-priced but non-performing buyers, the bank turned to us. We purchased the building for $10 million, which was only $27 per square foot.

Less than a year later, we bought the 36-story, 720,000-square-foot Harwood Center building nearby for $50 million, or $69 per square foot. At the same time, we began acquiring adjacent land, parking lots, and other downtown property.

Our reasoning was that this area of Dallas had been bad for so long that we believed it had finally reached the critical point where the community would step in and do something about it. Downtown needed commitments from the mayor, the city council, and the public at large to spend money on infrastructure and provide incentives to bring restaurants, businesses, and housing downtown.

At the time of these purchases, the city had begun to create some of these incentive programs and we were the first developer to work with the city to rehabilitate an old downtown office building for other uses. Our historic Kirby Building on Main Street was a beautiful landmark office tower that had been sitting empty for several years. We had decided to work with the city to redevelop it into high-rise apartments during the same time period that we also were buying newer office buildings. The Kirby's redevelopment process was extraordinarily difficult and mired in red tape, but it eventually turned out well for the city and for us. As we continued to acquire property, we believed more and more that this type of public-private venture could and would help downtown survive and eventually thrive.

About this same time, new transportation initiatives were being carried out. Light rail lines into downtown were planned, bringing pedestrians, commuters, and another type of vibrancy to the area. The Arts District, the cultural heart of Dallas, was also planning a large exciting expansion. It seemed as if the future for downtown Dallas was looking up and that momentum was about to be on our side.

As contrarians, we always strive to get in—and get out—ahead of the curve. As we expected, over the next few years there was much positive political and civic conversation and optimistic editorials written by respected journalists about how great things were going to be. There was a broad awareness of what was needed to revitalize the city's inner core and the momentum seemed to be increasing. We were optimistic about the future.

Office buildings in most other urban areas were doing reasonably well and other older office buildings in downtown were being converted to apartments. These renovations took some of the aging office supply off the market, slightly reducing vacancies. At the time there were no sale comparables for us to consider and it was hard to say whether the prices investors would pay were likely to go up or stay in the same range. But we felt comfortable that for the next several years momentum was going in the right direction.

In late 1997 and early 1998, however, we began to realize that many of the actions we thought were necessary to truly revitalize downtown Dallas were not happening. The will of the citizens wasn't there to complete the initiatives that had been started. Civic commitment seemed to have vanished and certainly our company alone could not turn things around. It was with some regret that we made the decision to sell before the positive momentum turned the other way.

We sold while the market was still optimistic. The winning bidder paid $110 million for the two buildings we had paid $60 million for just less than three years earlier. Our profit was $50 million. The sales price was the result of the optimism that still existed about downtown's future, as well as upgrades and improvements we had made to the properties. We had renovated the lobbies of both buildings, placed artwork throughout the common areas, raised the level of tenant services provided, and signed new leases at increased rental rates.

We wished the new owner well, unsure if we had sold too soon or not. But we weren't looking back. It wasn't long after that the momentum publicly stalled and the office market fell back into doldrums that were as bad as they were before our purchases. In fact, as of early 2003, no new high-rise office buildings have yet been built in downtown. We realize now that we timed the momentum on both our purchases and our sales almost perfectly. This is rare even for the most seasoned investors.

Despite our desires to make downtown Dallas better, we knew that there was a limit to how much we should invest with our heart. It is a good thing to let your heart take the lead every once in a while, but judgment and rational thinking should more often than not drive your decisions. We were fortunate to have sold when we did.

It is a good thing to let your heart take the lead every once in a while, but judgment and rational thinking should more often than not drive your decisions.

This example is just one more important lesson about how the critical nature of timing relates to success in real estate investing. Had we not let go of the buildings when we did—even though our hearts wanted to hang in until things got better—the buildings would probably be worth no more today than when we bought them. We would have missed an important $50 million opportunity.

What Does It Mean When We Say Positive Momentum Is "at Risk"?

Positive momentum is "at risk" when it is potentially topping out or facing a downturn. Slow upward movement in the real estate market doesn't necessarily indicate risk. Momentum can continue slowly and still not top out for quite a while. That makes it tricky to analyze. Momentum is not a simple thing.

However, when you analyze one specific situation, as we did in the case of St. Paul Place and Harwood Center, and see strong indications that momentum could change (in this case, the civic commitment was in jeopardy), the right decision is to sell. We were seeing more talk and less action, which told us our primary reasons for believing in continuing momentum were potentially faulty. We felt the whole idea of positive momentum for downtown Dallas was at risk and—although we couldn't know with any certainty—we feared the positive momentum would end abruptly.

When you analyze one specific situation and see strong indications that momentum could change the right decision is to sell

---

If you're concerned about positive momentum turning, the first thing to do is to check your original reasoning for buying and holding your property. If you look at the market and can't make the same analysis you did when you bought, as it relates to momentum, then you should consider selling. It's better to sell too soon than to take the risk of staying in a market that could sour.

In stock market terms, with St. Paul Place and Harwood Center we thought we were buying at the beginning of a new bull market in downtown Dallas. In contrast, in 1998 we feared that what we had hoped would become a bull market was really a bear market rally. Things were better in terms of perception and prices had come up on a per-square-foot basis, but the reality was not following as it should have.

Let me be quick to say that we could have been wrong. The downtown Dallas office market might have continued upward and we might have sold out leaving something on the table. For us, it is better to be safe than sorry.

Four Ways to Know Positive Momentum Is at Risk

1. **Prices on competitive properties stop going up or go down.** The bottom line to consider is price. If you have a large market with good data available, look to see if prices have stopped going up. For instance, if you are in a single-family home rental market, there will be multiple listing services with information on properties recently sold. If you start to see properties similar to yours available but with prices that are no longer escalating or, worse yet, are going down, momentum may have stalled and may be headed downward.

2. **The bid/ask spread widens.** If what sellers are wanting (asking prices) is substantially more than what buyers are willing to pay (bid prices), that means trouble. If the number of transactions slows down because buyers think properties are worth less than sellers are asking, then a gap is forming that could be dangerous. Either the buyers will change their minds because operations will prove the higher expectations of the sellers to be true or sellers over time will bring their prices down and the buyers get their way. The key is to note when the differences between asking prices and offers start to increase, which could indicate that positive momentum is about to disappear.

3. **The rental market softens.** If the rental market for your real estate deteriorates because of higher vacancies and/or lower rents, this is a strong signal that property prices could also soften. Depending on the reasons, the timing, and the likelihood of a continuing softness, this should be something for you to con-

sider as you continue to review whether or not the momentum is "at risk."

4. **Avoid the "pack mentality."** The real estate community is always full of gossip. Sometimes this free advice is worth something. Other times it's worth exactly what you pay for it. Listening too much to the marketplace can give you a bad case of "pack mentality" that might cause you to miss swings in momentum. Get different opinions and evaluate them not only for what they are but also for who said what and why.

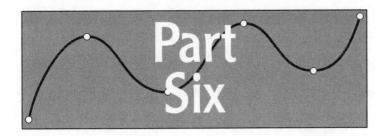

Part
Six

Putting Theory into Practice

Is Real Estate
the Next Bubble?

A s you might guess, traditional book publishing takes time. I'm writing these last chapters in mid 2003, many months before its release. What that means, of course, is that all of my perspective is colored by this moment in time. When the book comes out, much will have changed. Markets hate uncertainty and the world is an uncertain place.

I met recently with Mark Gibson, one of the founders of Holliday Fenoglio Fowler, a large financial intermediary for commercial real estate. We talked at length about where real estate stood from a timing perspective and where it was headed. Mark said simply in his best Texan drawl, "Real estate is the prettiest girl at the dance."

Now for those of you who aren't from Texas, let me try to translate. What Mark was saying is that the capital markets, whether for debt or equity, were putting vast sums of money into real estate in the spring of 2003. Real estate for the past few years, specifically since the 2000 stock market crash, had become the investment of choice, getting the lion's share of attention, much like the prettiest girl at the dance.

Mark and I both realized that what has been occurring is that real estate assets with dependable cash flows are being chased by both investors and lenders, creating a huge new flow of funds. The markets were driving capitalization rates down to levels not seen in the 35 years I've been in the real estate business. The most precious asset was a piece of real estate with positive cash flow and a loan that could be prepaid. In other words, a property that had either no debt or debt that could be refinanced with a modest penalty commanded the greatest value in the marketplace. Depending upon the type of real estate, cap rates were down to the 5%-7% range, instead of the 8%-10% range with which we all were familiar. These lower cap rates resulted in dramatic price increases.

Mark brought a chart prepared by the Federal Reserve Bank that showed a comparison of historical commercial mortgage flow of funds into or out of real estate. (See Figure 17-1.) I found the data staggering. Throughout the mid 1990s, mortgage volumes were growing but not at a great rate. In 1997, there was approximately

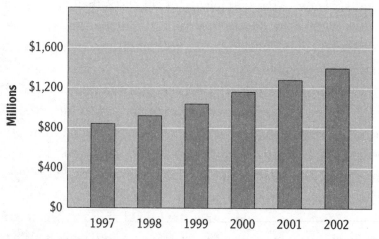

Figure 17-1. Historic commercial mortgage flow, 1997-2002
Source: Federal Reserve Board

Is Real Estate the Next Bubble?

$800 million in new commercial mortgages for all properties in the United States. By 2002, that amount was just under $1.4 billion and appeared to be growing into 2003. Clearly, for commercial properties from the standpoint of debt, real estate had become one of the most sought-after investments.

Even more extreme was the exponential growth of the flow of debt funds into the residential market, as Figure 17-2 shows. Many people I know have refinanced their homes two and three times since 2001. While the numbers clearly show that debt growth in real estate is huge, the demand from the equity side at all levels is equally robust.

It is interesting to see that some of this change, especially in the debt area, started before the decline of the stock market. However, I believe most of it was driven by the volatility that occurred in the stock market. The bursting of the giant stock market bubble in the spring of 2000 left many individual investors with shattered dreams and a desire for new, safer places to invest.

Perhaps even more important were the people controlling the investments of pension funds. The dramatic decline in proceeds from the stock market caused one pension fund committee after another to reevaluate allocations among stocks, real estate, and other invest-

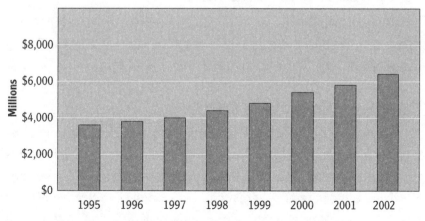

Figure 17-2. Flow of funds into home mortgages, 1995-2002

Source: Federal Reserve Board

ments. This has, in the last few years, caused an immense new flow of funds into real estate. This prompts us to ask both how long this will last and what it means to us as real estate investors.

Applying the Seven Trends

As I have stressed throughout this book, real estate is a local business—a belief that is underscored by the fact that four of the seven trends are local, property-specific trends. In this chapter, we are reviewing where real estate stands in a broad sense looking toward the end of 2003, without restricting our analyses by geographic area or property type. Because of this, there are obviously many exceptions to the general comments that I will make about how the trends are affecting the broad real estate cycles in 2003. As previously noted, huge differences in the effects of the trends always exist among property types and geographic locations.

> Real estate is a local business—four of the seven trends are local, property-specific trends.

The Three National Trends

We will now examine the three national trends we discussed in earlier chapters as of 2003 and their influence on the successful investment in real estate.

NATIONAL TREND #1: INFLATION

As you can see from Figure 17-3, inflation has been rather tame the last few years. In fact, many people fear that a period of deflation is coming. Deflation can be very disadvantageous to real estate. However, my personal belief is that, because of the effective Federal Reserve policy, we will not see a period of deflation, although it remains a realistic risk.

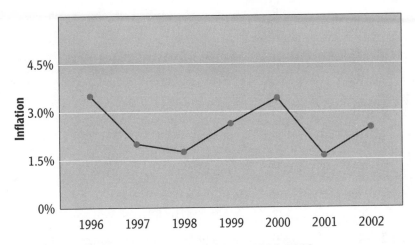

Figure 17-3. Historic national inflation rate, 1996-2002
Source: Bureau of Labor Statistics

As a trend affecting the real estate cycle, inflation at this point has been relatively less important than other trends. Depending on the money supply of the Federal Reserve and in time a reignition of inflationary pressures, this may change, of course, but in the very near term after 2003, I don't believe inflation will cause capitalization rates to dramatically rise or fall.

NATIONAL TREND #2: INTEREST RATES

In an effort to fight the dramatic slowdown in the economy that started with the bursting of the stock market bubble in the spring of 2000 that led to the recession in 2000-2001, the Federal Reserve responded aggressively by lowering interest rates. As Figure 17-4 shows, interest rates had gone from 6% in 1995 to 1.5% in 2002 in terms of the Fed Funds rate.

Perhaps even more interesting is that 10-year Treasuries have gone from 7% in 1994 to a low of 3.8% in 2003. These are unprecedented numbers.

It used to be assumed that 10-year Treasury rates would have a base of about 3.5%, excluding inflation, for a return that an investor would want. Then the balance over 3.5% would be what investors

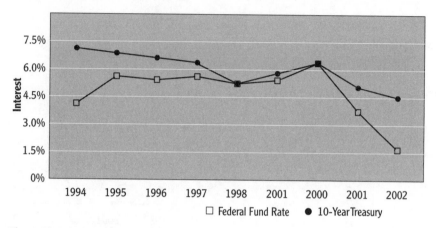

Figure 17-4. Historic federal fund rate and 10-year treasury rates, 1994-2002
Source: Dallas Federal Reserve

perceived inflation would be on average over the next 10 years. Using that rule of thumb, investors perceive that inflation will be well less than half of 1%—in other words, almost zero over the next 10 years.

I believe what this really shows is that people are investing in Treasuries and other traditionally "very safe" investments out of fear and uncertainty. I don't believe these low levels can be sustained.

I believe that people are investing in Treasuries and other traditionally "very safe" investments out of fear and uncertainty.

For now, the dramatic reduction in interest rates is one of the most dominant economic trends our economy is experiencing. When interest rates go down, generally cap rates go down. That historic relationship remains true for the real estate cycle at work in 2003. The dramatic decrease in interest rates is the unique factor at this time. This is part of the reason that there was a dramatic reduction in cap rates and that prices of real estate were generally rising.

NATIONAL TREND #3: FLOW OF FUNDS

In early 2003 I knew that real estate was the prettiest girl at the dance. My question was "How long would she continue to be?" It's difficult to analyze exactly how long the money flow will continue. We know it depends on how long the stock market stays down and how other investment opportunities behave. As I finalize this book, the stock market has moved well up off its lows and may have stabilized.

Analyzing timing in real estate markets is a dynamic process. I continuously evaluate flow of funds, because to me it's one of the most important keys to how far the current upward trend in prices goes. I'm not sure how long the flow can continue at these high levels.

Analyzing timing in real estate markets is a dynamic process. I continuously evaluate flow of funds.

If the money supply coming into the economy is growing at a healthy rate, this will help create a continuing flow of funds into real estate as well as other forms of spending. The Federal Reserve has pursued a policy of creating a healthy growth of money supply in order to fight the recession of 2000 and 2001 and the anemic recovery of 2002 and early 2003. Further, the unique geopolitical risks with terrorism, the war in Iraq, and continued uncertainty in North Korea further caused the Fed to keep interest rates low and keep lots of money available to the economy.

As Figure 17-5 shows, the money supply had grown on average $600 billion per year between 1999 and 2002. As long as this kind of growth continues, funds should continue to flow heavily into real estate.

The Four Local Trends

Let's now examine the four local trends and their influence on real estate investing.

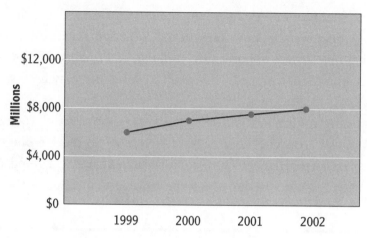

Figure 17-5. Historic M-3 money supply, 1999-2002
Source: www.econstats.com

LOCAL TREND #1: JOB GROWTH

The current analysis of job growth over the last couple of years reflected a major negative for real estate. As Figure 17-6 from the U.S. Department of Labor shows, the country in 2001 and 2002 had negative job growth. This would indicate falling NOIs and indeed NOIs have been going down.

When this happens, prices usually fall as well. However, what has been happening in 2002 and early 2003 is that cap rates have been falling faster than NOIs, moving prices up despite lower NOIs.

LOCAL TRENDS #2 AND #3: IN- OR OUT-MIGRATION AND PATH OF PROGRESS

These trends have more to do with specific properties in different geographic areas, so, for the purpose of this discussion of broad real estate cycles, they have little influence.

LOCAL TREND #4: NEW CONSTRUCTION

As a whole, new real estate construction slowed in 2000 through early 2003, and was not the problem that it had been in some cycles

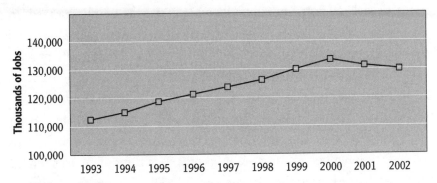

Figure 17-6. National job growth, 1993-2002
Source: Bureau of Labor Statistics

of the past. For instance, high levels of construction continuing far too long exacerbated the crash that devastated many real estate investors in the mid 1980s.

Throughout the country—in office markets, apartment markets, and (to a lesser extent) retail and hotels—vacancies are rising and rent is falling. Real estate gross income is under great pressure and may continue its fall in the near term.

Taking Stock of the Seven Trends

As of mid 2003, the seven trends are in conflict. The national trends, particularly interest rates and the flow of funds, have dramatically lowered cap rates and pushed prices up. The local trends, specifically job growth and new construction, have been a drag on price increases. As NOIs decrease, the amount of income being capitalized by the cap rates is at a lower level than it had been in years. This conflict of trends has resulted in rising prices even in the face of declining economics.

Anecdotal and Exogenous Events

Adding some additional anecdotal information, the situation looks even stranger. We are in a unique time in history, marked by the following characteristics:

- **Geopolitical fears.** On September 11, 2001, the world changed. In real estate markets since that time, premiums were paid for properties with quality cash flows and a lack of interest was seen in higher-risk, higher-profile real estate.
- **State and local tax pressures.** State and local governments are under great pressure financially and accordingly have been raising taxes. The tax increases on commercial real estate property have been dramatic. In good times these increases would be passed on to the tenants, but in 2003 in many cases there is no pricing power because vacancy rates are just too high. For example, our structured finance division was in final due diligence on a loan to a New York hotel when we found out that property taxes were about to go up $1 million. This lowered the NOI from $9 million to $8 million and, applying a capitalization rate to NOI, lowered the hotel's value by $10 million. Needless to say, we didn't make the loan.
- **Insurance costs.** Insurance costs have skyrocketed since 2000. Our apartment portfolio insurance costs in 2000 were 11 cents per square foot. In 2002, insurance costs had increased to 32 cents per square foot, almost three times previous levels. We were not unique. Insurance is up from a minimum of 50% to as much as 300% or more throughout all types of real estate in all geographic areas. These increases are due to the insurance companies' attempts to recover stock market losses and an increased volume of payments on claims in recent years.
- **Security costs.** Security costs, especially for commercial real estate, are a new and increasingly necessary expense. As a result of increased sensitivity to the threats of terrorism, security is now viewed as a necessity and, again, because of lack of pricing power in 2003, the cost of providing increased security protection is difficult to pass on to tenants.

Remember: Real Estate Lags Behind National Economic Cycles

Real estate often lags behind national economic trends, particularly on the demand side of real estate (job growth and migration). Whether this will be the case in decades to come or whether a new phenomenon will change the way we analyze real estate, we cannot say. But when the overall economy recovers, demand for real estate and ultimately inflation of replacement costs likely will follow. Still, the lingering effects of 9/11 and ongoing fear of terrorism could continue to increase costs and reduce NOIs, property values, and our standard of living.

But what about those low cap rates? Will they move back up as the economy recovers? This is a question we must continue to ask ourselves.

Has There Been a Paradigm Shift?

This section could be subtitled, "Is the United States Becoming More Like Europe?" Let me explain.

As Mark Gibson and I continued our philosophical discussion of real estate timing and where we were in the cycle, we wondered whether a permanent change has occurred and whether our country has become more like Europe in terms of how real estate investing is perceived. At the heart of our question is the issue of how long cap rates would stay at low levels. There is little question in my mind that NOIs will stabilize, but will this be at 10%, 20%, or even 30% below current levels? And once they stabilize, how fast will they improve? Does it make sense that people have been paying high prices for real estate while operating results are declining?

Two of the driving forces behind the current unusual marketplace are the very low interest rates and the ability of investors to finance properties. Paying a cap rate of 5% or 6% financed today with a five-year interest rate in the 3.5% range can result in an 8% or 9% cash distribution to an owner. Any pension fund manager who today is able to deliver a 9% cash flow over the next five years looks very good. Through structuring an investment appropriately in this very low interest rate environment, one can justify a low cap rate and relatively high purchase price for a property—and many people are doing so.

Consider this example. In Dallas a fairly modern and recently leased office building was sold in early 2003 at a little over $200 per square foot. Based on the NOI in place, this three- or four-year-old building was sold at a capitalization rate lower than 6%. Based on the financing over the next five years, the pension fund owners will receive a 9% return on their equity. That's the good news.

The bad news (or at least the question) is "What happens at the end of the five years?" The buyer paid over $200 a square foot for a building that could be built from the ground up for somewhere around $150 to $175 per square foot. More to the point, the Dallas office market in 2003 has a 25% vacancy factor, with 50 million square feet of space vacant out of a rentable total of 200 million square feet. Rents are going down, not up. In six years, when the loans come due and the owner has to refinance, will interest rates be the same, lower, or higher? I believe they'll be much higher. If interest rates are much higher and the NOI is lower or the same, where will the investment return go? What will the value of the building be if the owner wants to sell it at that point? These are complex and troubling questions.

Many of Mark Gibson's clients are struggling with the same issues. Some argue that real estate in the United States would become more like it is in Europe, where cap rates have remained low for a long time, and properties have generally been held for generations. Well-located property in Europe trades much less frequently than here and people hold property in a manner that respects a low but steady long-term return. In our country, we compare real estate to other forms of investments, such as stocks, and expect much higher returns than these European owners receive.

Some argue that real estate in the United States would become more like it is in Europe, where cap rates have remained low for a long time, and properties have generally been held for generations.

There are many good arguments for why interest rates and cap rates may stay down for a while. A lot has to do with whether or not inflation emerges and at what level. It's possible to foresee a period of extended low inflation that would not be harmful to real estate. In that environment, it would be logical to assume that we've entered a period where cap rates have made a more or less permanent change to a lower level and prices of real estate deserve to be higher.

Still, this is the United States, not Europe. Our quest for real estate has developed in a way that is tied to personal freedom and is fundamentally different from Europe, with its long history of royal ownership now given way to ownership by family dynasties.

This is the United States, not Europe. Our quest for real estate has developed in a way that is tied to personal freedom.

Is the Real Estate Bubble About to Burst?

In many ways, 2003 can be compared to the early 1980s. When the Reagan administration created tax incentives to encourage investing in real estate, to me it was a clear ringing of the bell that real estate was about to boom and be the place to invest. Similarly, when the stock market crashed in the spring of 2000, that was another bell-ringing event, suggesting that real estate was about to experience a huge influx of funds. Other factors making the bell ring even more loudly since 2000 are the dramatic lowering of interest rates by the Federal Reserve and the unprecedented decline in cap rates, particularly for properties being refinanced.

So as the real estate bubble gets larger, should we all hold our ears and get ready for it to burst?

So as the real estate bubble gets larger, should we all get ready for it to burst?

For residential properties, especially single-family homes, I don't think the bubble's in danger. The numbers and statistics suggest that prices will level off. There will, of course, be exceptions. In some markets, where prices have increased so rapidly, such as Sacramento, California, drastic price declines could be on the horizon.

On the commercial side, it's hard to say whether or not the excesses of 2000 through 2003 are enough to clearly suggest a bubble in danger of bursting. But if we don't soon see a leveling off of prices and increase in NOIs, conditions are ripe for another real estate bust. In the near term, as long as interest rates stay low and the flow of funds continues, prices are likely to continue in the final leg of the upward cycle. The real question is how far that leg will continue and to what extreme. If the flow of funds continues at high levels through 2005 and 2006, then the downward cycle is likely to be extreme.

One of the basic laws of nature in real estate is that it rarely makes sense to pay a price for existing real estate that is greater than the cost of replacement. What I'm seeing anecdotally in the market today, like the office building in Dallas I described earlier, is that investors are paying prices above the cost of replacement. This could be logical in high inflationary times when replacement costs are sure to be going up, but in 2003 prices of new construction have been falling.

What Should Investors Do?

In a nutshell, be thoughtful and apply the timing lessons of this book. There are some times when things seem so bad that I would say throw caution to the wind, be contrarian, and jump in. But 2003 has been a time when things on the surface seem good, yet the reality is that current pricing structures and interest rates seem unsustainable. So, as a buyer, I have been very cautious and selective.

One huge benefit of buying this year has been the availability of low interest rates. The key is to use the low-interest rate environment properly. Taking on floating debt or even five- to seven-year debt, in my opinion, will be a mistake. If, on the other hand, you bought a property in a low-interest rate environment and obtained a 10- or 15-year loan at a fixed rate, you would be maximizing the environment. Even though you would have paid a high price for the property, a lot of that price may be justified by the financing.

If you already own real estate financed at a higher rate, then it is time to consider refinancing at a lower rate or even selling. When the trends are at extremes, as they are now, that's a strong reason to get as much money out of real estate as possible. A combination of selling and financing should be the priority.

Throughout 2002 and early 2003, our company pursued a strategy of selling properties, refinancing, and deploying more assets into the structured finance lending business. With structured finance, we're looking for real estate in which conventional lenders are not interested—in other words, where the funds flow the least. First this was hotels, but we think in the future it will be office buildings and other types of commercial property. We believe that foreclosures will increase after 2003 and that, as NOIs go down, many properties with higher fixed interest rates from pre-existing mortgages will end up in default.

As I finish this book, it is too early to say with any certainty, but the real estate bubble may burst and prices may come down dramatically. This could provide for a dramatic buying opportunity for investors who are liquid, patient, and mindful of the timing. Further, even in a generally high overall real estate marketplace, if you use these timing strategies, there are always timing opportunities, given the wide range of real estate types and the countless individual submarkets.

Real Estate Timing: More Art Than Science

When I started out in real estate, all I wanted to do was own more and more property. I enjoyed driving around Ann Arbor counting the numerous "Hall Management Company" signs I drove by. Never mind the fact that I was losing money on many of those buildings; it just seemed like they were a part of me. It was as though I had a large trophy case with a collection of special butterflies in it.

In real estate, butterfly collectors lose. It's not a business that should be based on ego.

The problem is that, in real estate, butterfly collectors lose. It's not a business that should be based on ego. For me and, I think, for many others in the business, selling is very hard to do. The whole idea of having fewer apartment units the day after I sell a property simply seemed like a loss to me. I really valued my company based in large part on how many thousands of units we owned as we grew bigger and bigger in the early 1980s.

Perhaps the best thing that happened to me, at least in some ways, was my long financial struggle from 1986 through 1992. It caused me to deeply reflect on the importance of my business and my life. I learned that collecting real estate for ego's sake was a disaster of an idea. I had gotten caught up in the belief that my identity was tied to my business. Today I know that real estate is not life. Life is about far more important and lasting things, including relationships, the environment, art, and ideas.

Real estate is not life. Life is about far more important and lasting things, including relationships, the environment, art, and ideas.

Tough times taught me how to focus and organize my business for bottom-line financial results—to stop collecting butterflies and start making money. Bottom-line profits combined with an ethical and responsible way of doing business are the basic philosophies on which I rebuilt my business and my life.

Science Can Help but It's No Panacea

One of the things I really hate about many how-to real estate books is that they promise too much. And, on the other hand, some promise nothing at all. In this book, I've tried to strike a realistic balance. Nevertheless, let me emphasize again that the ideas in this book about the seven trends affecting capitalization rates and property NOIs and, in turn, the upward and downward cycles of real estate, are far from scientific theory. I believe these are important rules of thumb, but they don't provide all the answers—because real estate investing isn't a science.

Actually, one of the aspects of real estate that I like the most is its inefficient, unscientific marketplace. That's right—*inefficient*. The more a business can scientifically be put into exact formulas, the easier it is to replicate and thus the lower the profit margins would be. A completely scientific approach to business, in my opinion as an entrepreneur, also would not be much fun.

So don't be put off by the fact that not everything about real estate can be answered scientifically by applying the seven trends. A lot of good can come from understanding how certain laws of economics have affected wealth and property prices in the past. But when it comes to interpreting where a piece of real estate is in a cycle and where it might go, it's more art than a science.

Don't be put off by the fact that not everything about real estate can be answered scientifically by applying the seven trends.

Art Is Understanding the Changing Relationships Among the Seven Trends

The seven trends alone are not the only influences on real estate cycles, but they are strong ones. Clearly, from the history of past cycles, we have seen that some trends are dominant over others.

In the mid 1980s, one dominant trend was new construction. Overbuilding was a huge problem. That problem, combined with a high flow of funds from tax shelter investment money created by congressional laws in the early 1980s, led to a real estate bubble that burst in 1986.

Contrast that with 2003, when new construction is relatively less important. From a perspective of which trends are dominant in the cycle, as I write this book, flow of funds and interest rates lead the group. Each cycle has different dominant trends and different relationships among them.

Figuring out which of these trends is more dominant and how they relate to each other when they are acting in conflict is not something that can be fully quantified in simple terms. Doing this well is an art in the sense that it is constantly changing and open to inter-pretation. You have to develop a feel for how these relationships work and what unique aspects there are in any particular cycle. There is no question that history repeats itself, but it rarely repeats itself exactly. You have to learn to trust your gut instinct.

Figuring out which of these trends is more dominant and how they relate to each other is an art in the sense that it is constantly chang-ing and open to interpretation.

The "feeling" side of real estate timing can be developed by using the tools described in this book regularly and in conjunction with your own anecdotal review of evidence in any given market. Certainly experience will give you a better feeling for the business than merely reading this or any other book. There is no substitute for getting out in the marketplace and being involved in the business. Hearing other people's ideas and views can be the most helpful tools in sparking your understanding of the marketplace. I weigh and bal-ance what is said and learn from people all the time. Anecdotal infor-mation is always useful.

I believe that gut instinct is merely putting together experience and knowledge with confidence. You develop intuition by doing the work and nurturing confidence in your own abilities to rationally understand a market and come up with ideas and plans of your own.

Perspective and Humility

I mentioned in Chapter 1 that the autobiography of William Zeckendorf was a book that I had treasured when I was starting out in the real estate business as a teenager. In the 1960s Zeckendorf was probably the most successful real estate investor in the United States. He was the reason New York became home to the World's Fair in 1964-1965. He developed skyscrapers throughout the United States and other countries. One of his young staff architects was I.M. Pei, now world renowned for his designs. Everything about William Zeckendorf was grand. Unfortunately, in the downturn of the mid 1970s, he ended up in personal bankruptcy and lost virtually everything. Like typical real estate investors at the time, he had a portfolio of many highly leveraged assets when the market went into a severe downturn.

I followed Zeckendorf in newspapers and magazines while he was going through his bankruptcy and the worst of times. As he began to rebuild, he needed an office; he found a publishing company in New York willing to lease him space if he would write and let them publish an autobiography. It is that book that further inspired me about the possibilities and exciting things that could be accomplished in real estate.

You might imagine how excited I was when, in my mid 20s, I found out that my hero, William Zeckendorf, was coming to Southfield, Michigan. My office was located there at the time, and I was thrilled to be in the luncheon audience to hear him speak. For me to take the time away from work and buy a ticket to a lunch was a big deal back then.

I arrived at the luncheon with great anticipation. My excitement turned to dismay when Zeckendorf, who was probably in his 70s at the time, spoke not about how to get rich in real estate, but about art and how it enriches our lives. It made no sense to me. All he wanted to do was talk about art and I was certain I had been ripped off.

Life, however, comes full circle and my perspective has expanded. So, while learning about how to make money and focus on bottom-line profitability is definitely important, there are two other lessons that I would like to leave with you—they are truly the most important lessons I have ever learned.

The first is that William Zeckendorf was right. After 35 years in business, I have come to realize that what is enduring in life is art and, I would add to that, relationships. In the broadest sense, if any of us leaves a mark on the world, it is that we build relationships with people that add to the quality of our lives. And the quality of our lives is interwoven directly with our appreciation for visual and other forms of art.

If any of us leaves a mark on the world, it is that we build relationships with people that add to the quality of our lives.

With all of this in mind, I believe we need to build our businesses, invest our money wisely, and enjoy the fruits of our labor, but do it all while realizing there are more important things in the world than money and material things. A greater appreciation of this deeper worldview will actually help you succeed even more in the transient day-to-day battle of timing the real estate cycles.

The other lesson that I want to leave with you is that of humility. No matter how successful you are or how smart you think you are, there will come a time when your gut instinct, judgment, and even this book will let you down. Timing in real estate—just like in all of life—has a habit of surprising us every once in a while and just when we least expect it.

No matter how successful you are or how smart you think you are, there will come a time when your gut instinct, judgment, and even this book will let you down.

All we can do is keep trying. Learning, understanding, listening to others, working hard, and making the best decisions you can make will yield good results over time. On the other hand, as one of our apartment property managers used to say years ago, "It's better by luck than by design." Her joke, which has become one that I have held onto for years, was simply that sometimes we do the best we can and things don't work out, while at other times things work out in spite of us.

All of this is my way of saying maintain your perspective, keep your humility, and enjoy your real estate investing. Here's to the best of timing!

Index

Index

Index

Index

Index

Index

Index

Index